COMMON SENSE ATH

By Barry S. Goldb

Table of Contents

Dedication

For my philosophy professors at Brigham Young University (BYU). Whoever thought it was a good idea to teach impressionable young theists about logical thinking and questioning authority should probably lose his or her job.

Preface

A Note on Straw Men

A "Straw Man" argument is when somebody ascribes to another party a belief they do not actually hold (whether in whole or in part) and then proceeds to attack this belief, rather than attacking the things that the other party *actually* believes. This is often done intentionally as an underhanded debate tactic or in political advertisements, but it can also occur simply out of ignorance.

I am fully aware that, as I discuss the things I believe (or the things I *don't* believe, as the case may be) and contrast them with what theists believe, I run the risk of creating straw men as I argue against those theist beliefs. In fact, it is almost guaranteed, since religious beliefs come in a mind-bogglingly huge number of varieties and it is literally impossible to come up with any single valid statement describing what all theists believe. Except, perhaps, for the extremely nebulous and completely unhelpful "Theists believe in God."

All I can say in my defense is that the theist arguments and beliefs I present in the various essays within this book are based on what I personally believed at one point in time and/or what I have heard others state as their beliefs. I fully acknowledge that many theists probably don't believe all, or most, or perhaps even *any* of the views I ascribe to theists. But *some* theists certainly believe *some* of the things I discuss, and those are the theists I am addressing in my essays.

Prologue

This book consists of numerous essays I have written over the years in an attempt to explain why my non-belief in a god or gods of any sort is justified and wholly rational, especially in response to numerous claims and assertions from theists of all stripes who love to present arguments and supposed evidence "proving" the existence of the particular God in which they happen to believe.

Now, there are atheists out there who have advanced degrees in philosophy and can stand toe-to-toe with professional apologists who attempt use all sorts of subtle logical arguments to prove the existence of some sort of god or gods. I am not one of those atheists (although I do have an undergraduate degree in philosophy and have spent a good amount of time exploring various philosophical arguments for the existence of any sort of god or gods whatsoever).

There are also atheists out there with advanced degrees in a variety of different scientific fields, ranging from evolutionary biology to cosmology to quantum physics, who can likewise stand toe-to-toe with theists who claim that a creator god of some sort is the only possible explanation for such things as the complexity of design in nature and the origin of the universe itself. I am not one of those atheists, either (although I have tried to keep up with the latest scientific theories regarding evolution, cosmology, physics and other fields).

There are even atheists out there who have spent years exploring the history of various world religions and can go toe-to-toe with theists who claim that only those who have studied the original scriptural texts in their original languages and have a deep understanding of the cultural and socioeconomic of the people to whom the scriptures were provided can *really* understand what any given religion is actually all about, especially when it comes to the nature of the god or gods worshiped by that religion. And, no, I am not one of those atheists either (although I have tried to learn about the history of ancient civilizations where various world religions arose).

So, just what sort of atheist am I? And what makes me feel qualified to talk about the subject of god and gods apart from simply stating that I happen to not believe in Him (or Her or It or Them)? For that matter, what makes me feel that my lack of belief is even rationally justified and not, say, the product of willful ignorance similar to those who refuse to believe that the earth is round, the Holocaust occurred, humans have walked on the Moon, or the universe is many billions of years old, despite all the evidence that those things are real?

Well, the one important thing I have come to realize over the years is that one doesn't actually *need* to be an expert in philosophy or science or ancient religions or anything else in order to be qualified to talk about the subject of gods and to feel rationally justified in not believing in any particular god or gods. All that is really needed is a good solid dose of **common sense**.

"But wait," I imagine people saying, "we all know that common sense can lead us astray!" And it's certainly true that some people deny such things as quantum mechanics, anthropogenic climate change, special and general relativity and many other complex subjects simply because those subjects go against their "common sense" and are either just too hard to understand or lead to results that contradict their expectations. However, one key difference is that, unlike religion, experts in quantum mechanics, anthropogenic climate change, special and general relativity, etc., all tend to agree with each other on the core principles involved with those subjects. There aren't, for example, 4000 different competing explanations for quantum physics the way there are over 4000 different competing religions, each with a different understanding of God's nature and God's will. Another key difference is that these various scientific theories have allowed scientists to make *consistent* predictions about the natural world instead of just throwing up their hands and declaring that, say, "relativity works in mysterious ways."

So, where does common sense lead us when considering the existence of god or gods? Let me count the ways:

First and foremost is fact that the God actually worshiped by most people is supposed to be an all-powerful, all-knowing and all-loving being who actually *wants* us to know and follow His will in order to achieve some sort of eternal happiness and avoid eternal torment. This is why He has supposedly provided the various holy scriptures that provide the foundation of most world religions, talked to various prophets throughout history, etc. Given all of this, it therefore makes no sense whatsoever to claim that God's will is so esoteric and difficult to explain that only a select few people can ever *really* understand it. Nobody ever claimed that quantum mechanics was supposed to be easy to understand, but the same cannot be true of God's will. For more on this, see *The Hypocrisy and Hubris of Biblical Interpretation* on p.66 and *Is God's Will Simple to Understand?* on p. 72.

Second, humans are really, really fond of making stuff up and ascribing agency to inanimate forces (see *Why Do So Many People Believe in [a] God?* on p. 57 for some more thoughts on this). We know that people have been inventing gods to explain natural phenomena, to provide a hope of an afterlife, and to give a sense of fairness in an otherwise unfair world since the dawn of history. Humans have also invented ghosts, fairies, witches, leprechauns, werewolves and all sorts of supernatural beings throughout history. Given this known propensity to make stuff like this up, why should any particular religion's "God" be an exception? It only makes sense that a God belief is just another superstition.

Third, on a similar note, there are literally thousands of different religions currently practiced in the world today (and many more if you count ancient religions that have died out over time), and each religion has a different concept of exactly what God (or gods) is like and what we human need to do in order to please said God (or gods). And, not surprisingly, most people end up believing in the particular God that is worshiped by their family and/or by the culture in which they are born. And yet, despite the fact that most religious belief is purely a matter of when and where somebody happens to be born, believers of all stripes tend to be absolutely sure that *their* particular religion and *their* particular concept of God is the "one true" faith. Many will even use various arguments and types of evidence (including personal revelation) to "prove" the truth of their faith, despite the fact that people of other faiths use the same exact arguments and types of evidence to prove their faith. All faiths cannot be true simultaneously, but they can certainly all be false. For more on this, see *The issue Isn't "Theists vs. Atheists" but "Theists vs. Everybody Else"* on p. 61.

Fourth, the various philosophical arguments that try (and fail) to prove the existence of God completely miss the point. Whether they are trying to argue that God is somehow required since the universe needs a "cause" (see *A Response to the Cosmological Argument* on p. 86), that God must exist since God is defined (by us, of course) as the most perfect being imaginable and existence is more perfect than non-existence (See *A Response to the Ontological Argument for the Existence of God* on p. 100), that God must exist because the universe is too "finely tuned" for the existence of life for it to have happened purely by chance (see *A Response to the "Fine-Tuned Universe" Argument* on p. 96), or what have you, none of these arguments actually deal with the sort of God that most people actually worship (the all-loving being who answers prayers, performs miracles, provides us with objective morality, rewards the faithful with eternal life, etc.) And none of these arguments actually provide a scintilla of observable and testable evidence to support their claims. It is just common sense that arguments that eschew actual evidence in favor of clever wordplay and definitional sleight of hand are not worth anything.

Fifth, we know the natural world exists and that there are laws that govern how it operates. And we have learned enough about the natural world that we are now able to explain many, many things that were previously thought to be utterly inexplicable without looking for some "supernatural" source as an explanation. On the other hand, we have zero evidence whatsoever that anything supernatural either does or even *could* possibly exist in the first place, and therefore it makes no sense whatsoever to consider it as a possible explanation for anything. As a result, it only makes sense to believe that everything in the universe — including the origins of the universe itself — is governed by natural laws even if we don't currently know what all those laws are. This point explains why common sense also rules out the possibility of the so-called "Deist God" that created the universe and has just let it run its course ever since without intervening. Sure, such a God is *possible* and not actually contradicted by any evidence, but it's also *not necessary* and there's no rational reason to believe in it. For more on this, see *Which is Easier to Believe, that Life Was created by God or by Chance?* on p. 144, *God of the Gaps* on p. 78, *A Response to the Argument from Design* on p. 81 and *Why the Word "Supernatural" Is Meaningless*) on p. 55.

Sixth, most religions have very specific descriptions of what God has said and done and what He has promised to do. All of these things are testable claims, and a complete lack of good evidence to support those claims along with mountains of good evidence that refutes those claims is in itself evidence that refutes God's existence. Young Earth Creationists are fully aware of this fact, which is why they will ignore or reinterpret any evidence that contradicts a literal reading of the Bible. Most theists, however, just ignore the contradictions between observed reality and descriptions of God's actions and words. Once you've refuted all the evidence that supposedly indicates that the God you believe in actually exists in the first place, however, it's just common sense to abandon that belief. For more on this, see _Absence of Evidence IS Evidence of Absence_ on p. 25.

Finally, it is blindingly obvious that every description of God from every major world religion is the product of primitive and superstitious peoples who knew very little about the world in which they lived. People who thought the earth was flat and covered by a dome. People who thought the stars were holes in the fabric that covered the sky at night. People who thought that gods and angels lived in the sky and demons lived underground. People who had no idea what caused diseases or earthquakes or floods or any other natural phenomena. And every single argument offered by any theist today to try to justify why it's not wholly irrational to still cling to these ancient superstitious beliefs is nothing more than an attempt to stick a Band-Aid on a popped balloon.

Chapter 1.   Why I Am an Atheist

The glib answer to the question of "why I am an atheist" is to say it's for the same reason I don't believe in the existence of invisible pink unicorns or teapots orbiting the planet Jupiter. In other words, since there's no good reason why I *should* believe in these things, I shouldn't need to justify my *lack* of belief in them. And this answer is perfectly valid and true insofar as it goes.

One problem with this answer, however, is that – unlike invisible pink unicorns and interplanetary teapots – a lot of people currently believe in God (or at least some form of being that can be called "God"). Which is to say that it's not blindingly obvious to most people that there is no good reason to believe in God, and so my answer as to why I am in the minority probably does deserve a bit of fleshing out.

I will say that, in a sense, I have been an atheist all my life, despite having been raised in a fundamentalist Christian faith by my parents. [As an aside, I know that many people will object to my characterization of Mormonism as a "fundamentalist Christian" faith, but doctrinal differences aside, the important thing is that I was raised to believe in the existence of a personal God and the literal truth of the Bible (and other scriptures).] The thing is, despite being taught from an early age to believe in God, I was never able to wholly internalize that belief. I mean, I accepted that it "must" be true because it's what my parents believed and it's what I was taught at church, but there's a difference between accepting something must be true and actually *believing* it to be true. As I grew older and learned more about the world around me, I became very good at compartmentalizing my acceptance that God "must" exist to protect it from the lack of any empirical evidence for his existence and the increasing evidence that actually contradicted his existence.

Majoring in philosophy (even at a religious school like Brigham Young University) really opened my eyes in a number of ways. It taught me both about logical thinking in general and about the many different worldviews held by different cultures throughout history. And it made it harder and harder for me to accept that there "must" be a God simply because of what I was taught by my parents and teachers. Since that time, I have continued to use the tools I learned in my philosophy studies to analyze the various reasons why somebody *might* believe in God and all the reasons why such belief is not justified.

For me personally, it comes down to the realization of just how ridiculous it is to believe that this entire vast universe was created just for our benefit. It made much more sense thousands of years ago when people thought that stars were just lights in the sky and that the Earth really was all there was. Now that we know just how many billions of galaxies there are, each with their own billions of stars, it's pretty obvious that the notion of a personal God who created us and watches over us and pays attention to us and cares about us is just wishful thinking.

On top of that, of course, is all the scientific evidence that has been gathered over the years that directly contradicts almost everything stated in the scriptures, whether it be the Bible, the Book of Mormon, the Koran, etc. At most, you can look to scriptures as allegorical stories that (hopefully) tell you how to live a good life, but if they're not based on facts then there's really no need to worship anything described therein.

Think about Santa Claus. When you're a little kid with no knowledge of science, it makes perfect sense for there to be magical flying reindeer that can travel all over the entire world in a single evening carrying a magical sled filled with billions of toys. After all, that's what your parents told you and how else could those toys mysteriously appear under the tree? As an adult, however, it's hard to imagine that anybody (let alone you) could have ever been so naive and gullible. Not only is everything about the Santa Claus story impossible, but there are much more plausible explanations available for the gifts.

The final piece of the puzzle for me was the realization that people are very good at self-deception and that plenty of folks are probably 100% sincere when they claim to have had a conversion experience or "felt the spirit" or what have you. That's why so many people cling to so many different faiths.

So yes, the short answer is that I am an atheist because there's no good reason not to be one. The longer answer is what the essays collecting in this book are meant to express.

Chapter 2.   What Is Atheism

Whenever there is a discussion about atheism, there will inevitably be a disagreement about what it "really" means to be an atheist and whether or not atheism can or should be considered a "religion" or "belief system" of some sort. The following two essays address these points.

What Is an Atheist

Time and again there seem to be disagreements as to what, exactly, it means to be an atheist. Most *atheists* usually want to define atheism as nothing more than a **lack of belief** in any sort of god, while many *theists* want to define it as an **affirmative belief** that no gods exist or even some sort of **assertion** that no gods exist.

Often, the way somebody defines atheism depends on the particular agenda that person has when defining the term. Theists, for example, may be trying to rebut the assertion by many atheists that theists are irrational for believing in something without evidence by claiming that atheists also "believe" in something (*i.e.*, the nonexistence of God) without evidence. Atheists, on the other hand, may be trying to completely avoid providing any justification for why they don't believe in God.

The minimum requirement to be an atheist, however, really *is* just to lack a belief in any sort of god or gods or God. Which is to say that, to be an atheist, you don't *need* to hold any affirmative beliefs or make any additional claims with regard to God or gods. Now, from a practical standpoint, most atheists who go out of their way to engage with theists in order to rebut supposed "proofs" of God's existence *do* hold an affirmative belief in the non-existence of God instead of just merely "lacking a belief" in God. But such an affirmative belief is not *required* to be an atheist.

So, what is an atheist? An atheist is any of the following:

- Somebody who simply *lacks a belief* in any sort of god whatsoever is an atheist.

- Somebody who *affirmatively believes* there is no sort of god whatsoever is an atheist.

- Somebody who *lacks a belief* in any sort of god whatsoever, but is willing to admit there's *no way to know for sure* whether or not any gods actually exist, is an atheist.

- Somebody who *affirmatively believes* there is no sort of god whatsoever, but is willing to admit there's *no way to know for sure* whether or not any gods actually exist, is an atheist.

- Somebody who *lacks a belief* in any sort of god whatsoever and also believes that, if any gods actually *did* exist, *there would actually be a way to know for sure* that they did, is an atheist.

- Somebody who *affirmatively believes* there is no sort of god whatsoever and also believes that, if any gods actually *did* exist, *there would actually be a way to know for sure* that they did, is an atheist.

- Somebody who *believes so strongly* that none of the traditional gods worshiped by major world religions exist that he feels it is something *he knows as much as he can know anything*, but is willing to admit that there could possibly be some sort of totally useless "Deist" god that started the universe rolling and then completely failed to interact with the universe since then, is an atheist.

- Somebody who thinks the whole "Deist" god idea is just as unsupported by evidence as any other concept of God and *believes so strongly* that there is **no** sort of god whatsoever that he feels it is something *he knows as much as he can know anything*, is an atheist.

- And, finally, somebody who just really doesn't think anything about God or gods *one way or another*, who neither believes nor disbelieves and honestly just doesn't care one way or another, is an atheist. It's like asking people whether they think stamp collecting is the best hobby or not, and for some people it just isn't a meaningful question since they have never actually spent any time thinking about stamps whatsoever.

Or, to put it another way, a **theist** is somebody who believes in a god of some sort. If *that description does not apply to you*, regardless of what you may or may not believe, you are an **atheist**. Period.

No, Atheism Is Not a Belief System

One common claim that some theists like to make is that atheism is some sort of "belief system," presumably to compare it to their own belief system and to imply that both systems are therefore equally valid. Atheists usually respond by saying this is ridiculous since atheism is a *lack* of belief and therefore cannot possibly be a belief anything, let alone a belief system. Now, it's certainly true that calling atheism a belief system is ridiculous, but the reason is slightly more nuanced than simply "a lack of belief can't be a belief system."

As mentioned above, most atheists like to claim that atheism is nothing more than a *lack of belief* in God, while many theists like to claim that it's actually an *affirmative belief* that God doesn't exist. And, depending on the atheist, there's actually some truth to **both** views. Which is to say that, no matter how much some atheists want to deny it, there *are* atheists who strongly believe that God doesn't exist to the point where they are willing to claim that they *know* — as surely as they know anything — that God doesn't exist.

However.

HOWEVER!

Whether an atheist lacks a belief in God or whether they believe God does not exist, there is no way at all that this represents any sort of "belief system" whatsoever. There is simply no system involved, and it does not make up any sort of worldview.

Theists tend to have a belief in God as their foundational worldview, the lens through which they view all of life. Where did we come from? From God. Why are we here? God put us here to worship Him. Where are we going after this life? It depends on whether we obey God's will or not. Where did the universe come from? God did it. Why is there suffering in the world? God has His reasons. Why is nature so amazingly beautiful? Thank God ("How Great Thou Art")!

As a result, theists naturally assume that atheists must also have some sort of foundational worldview, some sort of lens through which we view all of life. And, since their worldview is based on a belief that God exists, our worldview must be based on a belief that God does not exist.

Except, this just is not the case.

If you ask atheists where did humans come from, they may have an answer based in current scientific theories or they may have no answer at all, but they won't just say, "We didn't come from God" as if that explained anything.

If you ask an atheist why we are here on earth, they may or may not have an answer, but they won't just say, "We weren't put here by God" as if that explained anything.

If you ask atheists what happens after death, they may or may not have an answer, but they won't just say, "It depends on whether we disbelieved in God" as if that explained anything.

If you ask atheists where the universe came from, they may or may not have an answer, but they won't just say, "God didn't do it" as if that explained anything.

If you ask atheists why there is suffering in the world, they may or may not have an answer, but they won't just say, "Because God doesn't exist" as if that explained anything.

And if you ask atheists why nature is so amazingly beautiful, once again they may or may not have an answer, but they won't just say "God didn't do it" as if that explained anything. The following essays discuss what constitutes "evidence" in the first place and where the burden of proof lies when it comes to providing such evidence.

Atheism Without Theism?

I was recently engaged in a conversation with a theist who kept trying to get me to acknowledge that atheists maintain that the billions of people throughout all of human history who believe in God were all wrong. This was obviously poorly veiled *argumentum ad populum* and I refused to play his game according to his rules. Instead, I kept pointing out that the majority of theists also maintain that the billions of people throughout all of human history who believe in God were all wrong, since they worship the wrong God, or belong to the wrong religion, sect, denomination, etc.

Every time he tried to argue that there must be something to this whole God belief if everybody accepted it except for a small percentage of atheists, I pointed out that every single theist was also part of a small group of people who disagreed with everybody else, so there's nothing special about atheists rejecting all other beliefs as invalid.

Well, after going back and forth like this for a while, getting more and more frustrated at my unwillingness to play his game and concede his point, he finally said something that just made my jaw drop in amazement:

> *What other people believe has nothing to do with the question asked. Deflection to what theists believe is nothing more than a rationalization. You don't base your atheism on what theists believe, do you?*

Seriously? SERIOUSLY???

I mean, I know that theists like to claim that atheism is its own belief system and all, but this is just ridiculous. Of course atheists base their atheism on what theists believe. That's the whole point! Atheism literally means "not theism" and is nothing more, nor less, than a reaction to and rejection of what theists assert to be true. Theists say, "There is a God" and atheists respond, "I don't believe you." If no theist ever talked about God in the first place, there would be no such thing as atheists. How can atheist know what it is that we don't believe in unless somebody else first tells us about it? Can you disbelieve in Santa Claus or Elves or the Loch Ness Monster if nobody has first told you what they are?

I dunno. I'm used to theists constantly trying to shift the burden of proof to make their arguments seem less irrational ("Atheists can't prove that God doesn't exist, so their belief in no God is just as faith-based as our belief in God"). And I'm used to theists constantly trying to portray atheism as some sort of "belief system" instead of simply a lack of belief. But it never occurred to me that somebody would actually complain that atheists dare to define their lack of belief according to what other people believe in.

Chapter 3. A Made-up Solution to Made-up Problems

I realize this is a gross over-simplification, but it occurs to me that religion and a belief in various gods are, at their root, just attempts at making up solutions to deal with equally made-up problems. Or, to put it a different way, religions frequently invent problems that do not actually exist in order to be able to claim that the particular deity worshiped by that religion (and not any other deities worshiped by other religions, of course) is the only possible solution to that problem.

For example, religious beliefs claim to provide the answers to the so-called "big questions" of life, such as "Where did we come from," "Why are we here" and "What happens to us after we die." But why do those questions actually *need* to be answered? Religions would have us believe that humans have an innate burning desire to know the answer to these questions and that "God did it" is the most obvious answer, but billions of people go through their lives every day without ever even wondering about those questions. And even for those who do consider those questions in their daily lives, "We don't know" is often a perfectly adequate answer. I mean, sure, it would be nice to know the answers, but it's not so important to most people that we need to just accept some made-up answer rather than remain in ignorance.

Similarly, religions would have us believe that (a) it's vitally important for everybody to understand what their "purpose" is in life and (b) their particular deity is the only thing that could ever possibly provide us with such a purpose. In reality, however, most people are perfectly capable of living a fulfilling and satisfying life without knowing what their "purpose" is, and those who *do* feel the need to have some purpose in life are perfectly capable of defining it themselves rather than needing one to be imposed upon them from some external source.

The existence of morality is another "problem" that religions try and use as a reason why their particular deity is so important and necessary. "Objective morality can only come from a perfect and all-knowing external source, so our deity is the only possible explanation for it." Except, of course, who said that humans actually *need* any sort of wholly "objective" morality in the first place? And even if we did need it, who is to say that it couldn't arise solely from, say, our own innate empathetic nature as members of a high social species and not from some wholly external source?

And then you've got free will. "Without God," theists will claim, "every aspect of the universe would necessarily be wholly deterministic and that would make free will impossible. Therefore, the only possible explanation for why we have free will is God!" Except, of course, who is to say that a universe without "God" would necessarily be wholly deterministic in every aspect? Chaos theory indicates, for example, that sufficiently complex systems may not be deterministic. And then there's the whole idea of quantum indeterminacy. Or perhaps free will actually *is* just an illusion after all and we just *think* we are freely choosing whenever we make decisions in our life. In fact, however, a universe *without* an omniscient God who knows in advance everything we will ever think or do seems a lot more likely to have free will in it than a universe *with* such a God.

And, of course, there are all of the rest of life's mysteries that science has not yet been able to explain. What caused the universe to exist? How is consciousness possible? How did life first arise from non-living matter? How did DNA evolve? Religions would have you believe that we all *must* know the answers to these questions and that they have the answer ("God did it," of course). But the reality is that, once again, most people are quite content to live their entire lives without ever considering such questions and have no trouble whatsoever not knowing the answers even if they do consider them.

I'm reminded of those late-night commercials that start out showing a bunch of weirdly incompetent people who cannot perform basic tasks in their lives like draining pasta without it spilling into the sink or keeping a blanket on their shoulders without it falling to the floor. You know — things that few people *actually* have trouble with on a regular basis. But once they've convinced you that these are *real problems* that *real people* have (even if they didn't realize it), they can then sell you the miracle product to solve this imaginary problem that you didn't actually have in the first place. Because that's how most advertising works — convince people they have a problem and then sell them the solution to that made-up problem. The only difference between this sort of advertising and religion, of course, is that those products actually exist even if the problems they solve don't.

Chapter 4.   Evidence 101

Many atheists love to claim that there is "no evidence" for any sort of god or gods whatsoever. Theists often respond that the lack of evidence isn't a problem, since (as the saying goes) "absence of evidence is not evidence absence." Many theists go even further, though, and assert that there *is*, in fact, plenty of evidence that their particular God exists and that it actually takes "more faith" to be an atheist since it requires ignoring all that evidence. The following essays explore what constitutes "evidence" in the first place and where the burden of proof lies when making claims.

What Constitutes "Evidence" of God

A common refrain from atheists, especially when asked to explain why they don't believe in God, is that there is just no evidence to support a rational belief in God. Not that there's no *proof*, mind you, but no *evidence*. And this seems to cause quite a lot of consternation for many theists who like to think of themselves as rational and who are quite convinced that there is, in fact, plenty of evidence to support their quite rational belief in God.

[Now, granted, there are *some* theists who are perfectly willing to admit there is actually no evidence for the existence of God, but they don't care since for them it's all about faith. But that's a topic for another day.]

So, how do we reconcile this conflict between the claims of evidence vs. the claims of no evidence? Surely, it's a binary proposition and there either *is* or there *isn't* evidence for God's existence, right? And therefore, one side must be right and the other side must be wrong, right?

Well, not quite. It all comes down to what somebody actually accepts as evidence in the first place, and this includes how one defines the term as well as how high or low you set the bar with your standard of evidence. It's probably better to say that atheists lack belief due to an absence of *good* evidence rather than an absence of *any* evidence, despite the fact that some atheists refuse to even concede this much and claim that any evidence that doesn't meet their standards doesn't even count as evidence in the first place.

Regardless of whether the issue is what constitutes "good" evidence or what can even be considered evidence in the first place, though, the underlying requirements are the same:

First, good evidence is **objective** in the sense that it is or can be experienced by anybody equally, given the same circumstances. As such, personal spiritual experiences do not constitute good evidence since, by their very nature, they are personal and cannot be directly experienced by others.

Second, good evidence can be **independently verified and replicated**. As such, so-called "anecdotal evidence" such as stories of miraculous occurrences and third-hand accounts does not constitute good evidence since they can't be verified.

Finally, good evidence provides **affirmative support** for a proposition and doesn't just attack supposed counter propositions. As such, any of the many supposedly logical arguments for the existence of God do not actually constitute good evidence for the existence of God insofar as they take the form of "Science doesn't have a comprehensive explanation for some phenomena (the origin of the universe, the origin of life on earth, the apparent design in nature, etc.) and therefore it's more likely that God did it." For more on this point, see *Lack of a Better Explanation Is Not Evidence for Your Explanation* on p. 27.

Again, some atheists will claim that any evidence that doesn't meet these criteria isn't "really" evidence at all. And some theists will claim that these criteria are arbitrary or unimportant and their "evidence" is just as valid. But the point of this post is to point out that when theists and atheists argue about evidence they may not actually be talking about the same thing.

Having said all that, here are some examples of the sort of things that many theists put forth as evidence for the existence of the particular god they happen to believe in and why none of it is what an atheist would consider to be "good" evidence (or, for that matter, why theists themselves would not consider it to be good evidence if offered to support the existence of anything other than the particular god they happen to believe in, including the gods worshiped by other theists). Inevitably, whenever a theist of any stripe claims that there is abundant evidence for the existence of the particular god they happen to believe in, this evidence turns out to be one or more of the following:

- The result of being told from birth by their parents and members of their cultural group that one particular god is the One True God™ and that one particular religion worshiping that One True God™ is the One True Faith™. Which, of course, means absolutely nothing as far as evidence goes else every single believer of every single faith would be equally justified in claiming that they had evidence that *their* god and *their* faith were true while everybody else's god and faith were wrong, which is a logical impossibility.

- Stories written hundreds and even thousands of years ago for which there is little (if any) supporting evidence (archaeological or otherwise) and plenty of contradictory evidence.

- A belief that if a prophecy written in one part of a book is said to have come true in another part of the same book, that this somehow means it *actually* came true instead of just meaning that somebody *claimed* that it did.

- A *post hoc* (literally "after the thing") reinterpretation of passages contained in their holy book done *after* a particular scientific discovery is made that lets them claim that, despite the fact that plain language of that passage either has nothing whatsoever to do with the scientific discovery or else is just plain wrong, this passage somehow miraculously matches that scientific discovery exactly (if you interpret the language *just* right, ignore the bits that clearly don't agree, and squint *really* hard). Strangely enough, however, there never seem to be any instances where somebody figured out the "correct" interpretation *before* science made the discovery.

- Lots and lots of anecdotal stories from people, both ancient and modern, who claimed to have had "miraculous" experiences, ranging from direct encounters with divine beings to inexplicable healings (never the restoration of a severed limb for some reason, though) to things as mundane as finding their lost car keys after praying for help. Aside from the fact that many of these stories might be outright fabrications, and aside from the fact that "inexplicable" is not the same as "miraculous," and aside from the fact that these events never seem to be repeatable in any consistent manner, and aside from the fact that accepting these stories as "evidence" of the divine means ignoring all the instances where prayers were *not* answered, once again we are faced with the fact that if such stories *were* actually considered evidence of the divine, then it would mean that there would be simultaneous evidence for the gods worshiped by completely different religions, since they all tell miraculous stories to support a belief in the existence of their particular god. And, once again, that would be a logical impossibility. Either these types of stories *are* reliable evidence, in which case all gods and all religions are simultaneously true (despite the fact that many claim that they are the One True Faith™), or else this evidence isn't reliable after all. And since the first option leads to a logical impossibility, the second option must be true.

- Personal spiritual witness. Sadly, the same exact logic applies here. People of different faiths worshiping different gods all claim to have the same sorts of personal spiritual witnesses, and if the same evidence can be used to prove completely conflicting results, it's not good evidence. Besides, personal spiritual witnesses are wholly subjective to the person having them, which means that there's nothing clear and obvious for atheists to "deny" since they aren't the ones who had the experience. To an atheist, it's just another anecdotal story.

- A conviction that if "science" cannot currently explain one or more aspects of observed reality, whether it be how the universe came to be, the origin of human consciousness, the complexity of DNA, etc., the only possible explanation is that the particular god worshiped by that particular theist (and not the gods worshiped by other theists, of course) is responsible for it. And it doesn't matter how many things science eventually is able to explain — there will always be *something* that theists can point to and say, "Well, what about *that*? Huh? Huh? Huh?" Again, however, this is not actually evidence of any particular god. It's just one big "Argument from Ignorance" that doesn't even demonstrate that the particular god the theist worships could even *possibly* exist, let alone actually *does* exist. You can't argue that your god is a "more probable" explanation for something until you can first demonstrate just how probable the existence of your god is in the first place. And, I'm sorry, but once you start talking about gods that supposedly exist "outside of time and space" (whatever the heck *that* means) and that are composed of "pure spirit" (whatever the heck *that* means) and are simultaneously all-powerful, all-knowing *and* all-loving (despite the inherent contradictions of such a being given all the suffering in the natural world), I'm afraid you've already lost that battle.

- Flawed pseudo-logical arguments that attempt to prove some general concept of some sort of supreme being (not the actual specific god worshiped by anybody, mind you) by relying on carefully crafted definitions and unwarranted assumptions. Even if it were true, for example, that the universe had a "cause" of some sort to exist, that doesn't mean that this "cause" is necessarily a god and certainly not the particular god you happen to worship. And just *defining* the particular god you happen to worship as "the most perfect being imaginable" and then claiming that a god that exists is more perfect than one that doesn't, doesn't mean that this definition actually reflects reality, any more than defining god as a chair means that the god actually worshiped by anybody must exist.

Absence of Evidence IS Evidence of Absence

It has often been said that there is no way to prove a negative and therefore it is impossible to ever prove that God does *not* exist. Or, as it is often phrased, "absence of evidence is not evidence of absence." In fact, however, as an atheist I am not trying to prove the non-existence of God. At most, I am trying to disprove his existence, which is a whole other kettle of fish as far as I'm concerned. Or, to put it another way, absence of evidence is evidence of absence when the evidence required to prove something is missing.

Let's say, for example, I claim that a full-size adult African elephant is living in my backyard tool shed. If such a thing were true, there would *necessarily* be certain evidence of the fact. I would need to have, for example, an unusually large tool shed at the very least. You would expect to hear the occasional trumpeting sounds at odd hours of the day and night. There would be some indication that large quantities of hay were being delivered and that copious amounts of waste products were being removed on a regular basis.

A certain elephant-y smell would be unmistakable as it wafted through the air. And, above all, you would expect to actually see the elephant if you opened the door and looked in.

Keeping all that in mind, the fact that my tool shed is barely five feet wide would be an indication that maybe I don't have a full-size elephant there after all. The fact that nobody has ever heard, smelled or seen the elephant would be telling, as would be the fact that there is no indication of any hay deliveries or waste removal going on. In sum, the lack of all the evidence of an elephant **that should be there** is conclusive proof that I do not, in fact, have an elephant in my shed. Unless, of course, I want to argue that my elephant is a magical, invisible, shape-changing elephant that subsists only on air, excretes only sunshine, is very shy and hides in another dimension whenever anybody opens the door. In which case, the only proper response is that the creature I have described can't even properly be called an elephant in the first place assuming it even exists.

The same logic applies with regard to disproving the existence of God. If God exists – at least the God as described in various scriptures and actually worshiped by those who claim to be religious – then there would necessarily be specific evidence of his existence. All prayers offered to God in faith would be **granted**, for example, since this is what the Bible explicitly promises ("granted," mind you, and not just "answered"). Prophecies made in God's name would unequivocally and unerringly come to pass in exactly the way they were prophesied to occur. Miraculous events performed by God, including the creation of the entire universe in six days, the flood in Noah's time, etc., would all be verifiable by modern science instead of being completely contradicted. And yet, time and again, every place where there *should* be evidence to support the existence of God, it is mysteriously lacking.

Of course, some would argue that God's existence requires no evidence because God is an immaterial being that exists wholly outside space and time and that once he created the universe he has had no interaction with it or us ever since and doesn't expect us to worship or fear or obey or even acknowledge it in any way. I cover this so-called "Deist" God later on in this book (see _Sorry, Deists — Your God Doesn't Exist Either_ on p. 125).

Lack of a Better Explanation Is Not Evidence for _Your_ Explanation

Time and again we see theists offering as evidence (or even as "proof") for the existence of a god of some sort the supposed fact that science is unable to explain something. Whether it be the origin of the universe itself, the origin of life on this planet, the apparent complexity of life, the existence of consciousness, or what have you, the argument is made over and over (and over) again that this supposed inability of science to explain something somehow "moves the needle toward," "provides evidence of" or even "proves the existence of" some sort of creator or designer.

Now, aside from the fact that most people who make these sorts of assertions are typically ignorant as regard to what science actually _says_ about the supposedly inexplicable mysteries and are instead just parroting talking points they have heard from other theists, the crucial point that gets ignored by these people is that the simple fact (if true) that science cannot currently explain something, whether it be the origin of the universe, the origin of life on earth, how consciousness works, or what have you, does not, by itself, in any way whatsoever "point to the existence of a creator," **since we have absolutely zero independent evidence whatsoever that a "creator" actually exists or even _could_ exist**.

Claiming that our inability to explain something is somehow evidence of some _other_ explanation for which there is no independent evidence is the very definition of the so-called "Argument from Ignorance" fallacy. For example:

"I saw a shadowy figure out of the corner of my eye that science can't explain — it *must* be a Ghost!" Wrong, unless you can first show that ghosts *do*, or at the very least possibly *could*, exist. If you have no independent evidence for ghosts, there's no way that ghosts can be the best (or even a possible) explanation.

"I saw a light in the sky moving in a manner that science can't explain — it *must* be an alien spacecraft from another star system!" Wrong again, unless you can first show that aliens from other star systems *are*, or at the very least possibly *could* be, visiting our planet. If you have no independent evidence that aliens from other star systems are visiting us, then there's no way that aliens can be the best (or even a possible) explanation.

"Life originated on earth some 3.5 billion years ago and science can't explain how it happened — it *must* be the result of God who created the universe!" Wrong, wrong, wrong, unless you can first show that such a creator *does*, or even possibly *could*, exist in the first place. If you have no independent evidence for such a creator, there's no way that a creator can be the best (or even a possible) explanation.

Etc., etc., etc.

To reiterate, **lack of an explanation cannot, by itself, be evidence for some *other* explanation if that other explanation has no other evidence to support it.**

On a related note, those who assert a god of some sort as the best explanation for something fail to understand that they are actually just offering a proposed **answer** to the problem and not actually an **explanation**. If "God did it," how did He do it? Where did God come from? What is God made of, if not matter or energy? What does it actually mean to exist "outside of space and time"? What is it, exactly, about God that lets Him be the "Uncaused Cause" or "Prime Mover"? Saying "God did it" doesn't lay out the mechanism by which it was done or the processes involved. It doesn't describe the physical laws that had to be followed. It doesn't make clear how a supposed being who exists outside of time and space, who is supposedly composed of neither matter nor energy ("pure spirit" or "pure mind") could possibly exist in the first place, let alone how it could interact with the material world and do all the things it supposedly did.

No explanation, just an assertion that leads to lots of additional unanswered questions.

The Probability that God Is the Best Explanation for Anything

Previously, in <u>Lack of a Better Explanation Is Not Evidence for Your Explanation</u> on p. 27, I discussed the idea that if you want to prove that your particular explanation for something is correct, you need to do more than simply point out that other explanations are flawed. You need to actually produce some evidence to independently support your explanation as well. One additional point that I think needs to be made, though, is the fact that in order to claim that your particular explanation for something is *more probable* than other proffered explanations, it's not enough to show how improbable those other explanations are. You need to actually show how probable *your* proposed explanation is in order to compare it to those other explanations.

If we *assume* as a given that God (let's say the God of the Christian Bible for the same of simplicity) exists, then it makes perfect sense to discuss whether it's more probable that God is the explanation for a particular phenomenon. If we *assume* that God exists, we are then perfectly justified debating whether, say, it's more probable that God is responsible for the diversity of life on earth or whether it's more probable that it is due to the operation of wholly natural processes.

But to *assume* that God exists renders any argument used to argue for his existence wholly circular and thus invalid. Before you can say that God is a more probable explanation for anything, you need to first establish the probability of God existing in the first place. In other words, you have to show that the possibility of God existing is non-zero before arguing that God is the best or "more probable" explanation.

When arguing that God is the "best" or "most probable" explanation for things like the existence of life in the universe or the complexity of some observed biological function like the human eye, theists like to toss out truly staggering numbers to show just how improbable it would be for these things to happen "just by chance." Now, what if we ignore the fact that most of these numbers are either wholly made up, ignore the fact that "according to the operation of natural laws" is not the same thing as "just by chance" and/or make the unwarranted assumption that starting conditions could possibly be any different than what they were? Let's say that theists are absolutely correct and the odds of, say, the human eye evolving "by chance" are some ridiculous number like 10^{200} to 1. Fine. So that's pretty damn improbable, right?

OK, so now, please tell me what the probability of God existing is so I can compare probabilities. Come on, just what are the odds that some sort of timeless, spaceless, immaterial, intelligent "being" of some sort who created the universe and did some or all of the things he is described as doing in the holy book of your choice actually does, or even *could* possibly exist. How probable is this God who is supposedly *more probable* than the alternative explanations?

crickets

False Equivalency and the Burden of Proof

Time and again theists argue that, since atheists claim that God doesn't exist, it is actually the atheists who have the "burden of proof" to show that God does not exist as they claim. When this happens, most atheists respond by saying that atheists in general "merely" lack a belief in God (or gods) and that they don't actually make any claims that need to be proven. Theists, they say, are the ones who go around claiming that God does exist, and atheists simply say, "I don't believe you" or perhaps even, "You have not provided me with any good reason, any compelling evidence or argument, to accept that your claim is true."

Now, this is certainly true as far as it goes, but it often comes across as just a way to avoid the burden of proof by putting it back onto the theists without actually contributing anything to the discussion aside from saying, "I don't have to prove anything, you do!" And some atheists take this a step further by actually acknowledging that atheists would indeed bear the full burden of proof of establishing that God does not exist if, in fact, they actually asserted that He didn't exist instead of just stating their lack of belief.

Well, this is all well and good for atheists who really do just lack a belief in God, but it makes those of us who actually assert that no gods actually exist seem a bit irrational (which is, of course, exactly what the theists have in mind when making their claim about the burden of proof in the first place). Are we irrational to assert that no gods exist? Perhaps, but there are two important things to understand here:

First, "absolute proof" only exists in the realm of pure mathematics in the first place, and the best anybody can ever actually be expected to provide is compelling evidence of whatever it is they happen to be asserting as true. Many theists actually seem to acknowledge this fact by claiming that the existence of God can neither be proved nor disproved (as a way of avoiding their own burden of proof) right before attempting to shift that supposedly impossible burden of proof onto atheists. Yes, they want to have it both ways: "God's existence can be neither proved nor disproved, but it if it could be then it would be the atheist's responsibility."

Second, while the "burden of proof" is on the person making a claim about something, not all burdens are equally onerous! In other words, there is a false equivalency in asserting that the burden of proof of somebody claiming there is no God is exactly the same burden of proof of somebody claiming there is a God.

Let me address these two points individually.

1. Can the Existence of God Be Proved or Disproved?

Is it actually the case that the existence of God can neither be proved nor disproved? Well, again, if you are talking about "proof" as in the absolute certainty only available in the realm of pure mathematics, then of course it is true. But that's not really what most people mean when they talk about proving something. If asked to prove whether I have an apple in my hand, I can do so for all practical purposes by opening my hand and showing the apple that I'm holding. Nobody claims that the apple could just be an illusion, that perhaps our whole existence is merely a dream or a simulation. When somebody asks me to "prove" that I have an apple in my hand, they are merely asking for compelling evidence that I have an apple in my hand, and I can provide that compelling evidence simply by showing the apple.

Similarly, if asked to prove that I don't have an apple in my hand, once again I can provide compelling evidence simply by opening my hand and showing that it is empty. This is what most people mean and expect when discussing proof in everyday life, and requiring something beyond compelling evidence when discussing the existence of God is nothing more than a dodge on the part of those people who know full well that they cannot provide any compelling evidence for their assertion. So the real question is not whether the existence or nonexistence of God can be "proved" but instead whether any compelling evidence can be provided as to its existence or not.

2. Is the Burden of Proof the Same between Theists and Atheists?

So, just how heavy is the burden of proof when it comes to providing compelling evidence for the non-existence of God and is it really the same as the burden of proof when it comes to providing compelling evidence for the existence of God? The answer to this can be summed up in a phrase made popular by the astronomer Carl Sagan, to wit: "Extraordinary claims require extraordinary evidence." When somebody makes an extraordinary claim (such as, say, that there exists an omnipotent, omniscient, and all-loving intelligent being who created the universe, appeared before various people, provided moral guidelines, performed all sorts miracles, made lots of promises about future events, etc.), the burden of proof becomes extraordinarily high.

It's not enough, for example, to simply provide an argument that suggests that something must be responsible for the formation of the universe or to claim that, since "science" can't currently explain some aspect of the natural world that therefore the particular God somebody happens to worship "must be" (or even "possibly could be") the actual explanation. It's not enough to point to anecdotal stories of people who occasionally received something they prayed for (especially when ignoring all the times they didn't get what they prayed for). It's not enough to point out cases where holy scriptures written by ignorant and superstitious Bronze Age desert tribesmen supposedly mention something that, if interpreted in just the right way, kind of, sort of reflect knowledge that people living at that time may not have been able to discover on their own (especially when ignoring all the rest of the text that completely disagrees with what we now know about the universe). Theists who claim that God exists have a very, very large burden of proof to provide compelling evidence that the God that they actually worship (as opposed to some sort of "hidden" God who created the universe and is now wholly imperceptible by any means) does, in fact, exist.

And what of the burden of proof for those of us who claim that no such God exists? Given the extraordinary high burden of proof theists bear in the first place, all we need do is point out that the sort of God actually worshiped by theists would necessarily leave behind plenty of compelling evidence of its existence, which means the lack of any such compelling evidence is, in itself, compelling evidence that such a God does not exist (see <u>Absence of Evidence IS Evidence of Absence</u> on p. 25). If further compelling evidence is required, we need only point out the logical contradictions inherent with the theistic concept of God in the first place (see <u>The Logical Impossibility of God</u> on p. 150).

Now, keep in mind that atheism does not exist in a vacuum, but is instead a response to a claim made by theists. Atheists didn't just come up with the idea one day that "no gods exist" and then start running around telling everybody this. Instead, it was theists who made the original claim that gods do exist and then tried to covert everybody else to their belief. Which is to say that, even if an atheist does bear *some* burden of proof for claiming that no gods exist, that in no way removes the much larger burden of proof that theists bear.

Another thing to keep in mind when weighing the relative burden of proof is that there's a difference between denying something for which there is compelling evidence and denying something for which there is no compelling evidence. If somebody claimed, for example, that the moon was an illusion and didn't really exist, then that person would bear a pretty hefty burden of proof to back up that claim since there is plenty of well-accepted evidence that the moon does, in fact, exist (we can see it, we have measured how it affects the tides, we have actually landed on it, etc.). Compare that with somebody who responds to a claim that a 10-mile wide cloaked alien spacecraft is currently hovering over downtown Manhattan, poised to obliterate the Empire State Building, by claiming that no such craft exists because there is absolutely no evidence of it even possibly existing (let alone actually existing). Sure, the person denying the existence of the moon and the person denying the existence of the cloaked spacecraft are both making a claim, but the burden of proof is not equal between these two claims. Similarly, atheists are not in the position of denying something for which there is compelling evidence, but instead in the position of denying something for which there is no compelling evidence, and as a result their burden of proof is much less than theists would have us believe.

Some theists, by the way, attempt to wiggle out of their burden of proof by saying that they merely "believe" in God without actually "claiming" or "asserting" that God exists (much the same, supposedly, as how many atheists claim that "lack of belief in God" is not the same as "asserting that God doesn't exist"). Sure, there are undoubtedly some theists who don't actually claim that God exists just as there are some atheists who actually do claim that God does not exist, but the typical dynamic is for theists to claim that God does, in fact, exist (and they have evidence and arguments to prove it), since most theists apparently understand how irrational it would be to believe in something you don't actually claim exists in the first place. Seriously, how ridiculous would it be to go around saying stuff like, "I believe that grass is green and rain is wet, but I'm not actually claiming that grass is green and rain is wet"?

The point of all this is that many atheists have allowed themselves to be convinced that the "burden of proof" is a bad thing that should on no account ever be accepted when it comes to the existence of God, and this just allows theists to claim that, while it may not be possible to prove that God does exist, it's just as impossible to prove that God doesn't exist and therefore atheists are as equally irrational as theists for believing in something that cannot be proved. Once we realize, however, that "proved" in this context just means "has compelling evidence to support" and that the burden of proof on theists is significantly higher than that on atheists, we should stop being afraid of the burden of proof and feel confident asserting without reservation that no God of any sort worshiped by anybody actually exists.

An Experience Is not the Same as An Explanation

Many theists are more than willing to admit that they have no evidence to offer to support a rational belief in their particular deity or the truthfulness of the teachings of their particular religion. "God's existence can neither be proved nor disproved," they will claim, and it somehow becomes a badge of honor in their minds to have "faith" in their particular deity despite a lack of evidence that it exists.

Other theists, of course, know just how irrational it is to claim to believe something without evidence (especially something as extraordinary as the specific deity they worship), and therefore they claim to have all sorts of evidence that their particular deity exists. Most of this so-called "evidence" is easy to dismiss out of hand, of course, as the sort of thing that wouldn't even convince *them* of anything if it was offered as evidence of anything apart from their particular deity. Things like anecdotal evidence, ancient stories written thousands of years ago filled with descriptions of magical events, unsubstantiated claims of miracles and more arguments from ignorance ("Science can't explain X, therefore my answer is the only possible explanation") than you can shake a Bible at.

But one particularly pernicious form of "evidence" that sometimes gets offered to support a belief in a particular deity is "personal spiritual experience." The argument typically goes something like this (as stated by one particular theist to me in a discussion):

> If I experience something first-hand, it is absolutely rational for me to believe in it. If I can't reproduce that experience for you, it is rational for you not to believe in it. In that situation, we are both acting rationally. But claiming that you know that I have not actually experienced what I have claimed - without any contrary evidence - is irrational, and even hypocritical.

And, yes, it is certainly true that I cannot rationally just claim that people have not experienced what they say they have experienced. I mean, sure — they *could* be lying about it, but the mere fact that I disagree with them doesn't in and of itself mean that I am right and they are wrong.

What arguments like this completely ignore, however, is that there is an important difference between *experiencing* something and knowing what the *explanation* for that experience is.

For example, if I see a light moving erratically in the night sky, it would be perfectly rational for me to claim to "know" (insofar as I can "know" anything in this world) that I saw such a light. Even if others claimed to have been looking at the same part of the sky at the same time and not see anything, I would still be justified in claiming to know that I saw it. The problem comes, however, when I then claim to also "know" that the *explanation* for that erratically moving light is that it was a spacecraft piloted by a highly advanced technological alien species from another star system, despite the fact that everything we know about physics proves such a thing to be impossible. I "know" I saw a light in the sky, but that doesn't mean I can also claim to "know" that the light was an alien spacecraft simply because I "experienced" it with my own two eyes. What I "experienced" was a light — I *assumed* what the explanation for that light is.

It's the exact same thing with personal spiritual experiences. When somebody claims to have heard a voice in their head or have felt a "burning in their bosom" or have had a sudden sense of calm and peace or awe or joy or what have you, the likelihood is that they really *did* have such an experience. I mean, sure, they *could* be lying, but assuming they really experienced what they claimed to have experienced, it's perfectly rational for them to believe that they experienced it. Just like it's perfectly rational for me to believe I saw a light moving erratically in the night sky.

The problem comes when theists go on to assume that the explanation for their experience is the particular deity they happen to believe in and then conflate the two things and claim to have directly experienced their deity. No, sorry — they may "know" that they heard or felt whatever it was they heard or felt, but that doesn't mean they can rationally claim to "know" that the voice or feeling was sent by their particular deity simply because they heard or felt it. What they *experienced* was a voice or feeling — they *assumed* what the explanation for that voice or feeling is.

Interestingly enough, those who claim that personal spiritual experiences are a perfectly valid reason to believe in their particular deity run into a wall of solid hypocrisy when faced with claims by theists of *other* faiths who have had their *own* personal spiritual experiences that they claim support *their* conflicting beliefs. On one hand, how dare an atheist assume that their personal spiritual experiences are mere delusions:

> *It is amazing what you can argue when you begin with the assumption that all experiences to the contrary must be "delusion" even when you have zero evidence of actually showing that your premise is true and that contrary claims are therefore delusion.*

And then, on the other hand:

> *What I know is what I have experienced. Those who make contradictory claims are lying, delusional, or mistaken.*

Even if it were true that atheists have "no evidence" that God doesn't exist (apart from the complete lack of evidence that should be there if it *did* exist), the fact remains that believers in other faiths claim to have the exact same type of evidence to support their beliefs as theists like the one quoted above claim to have to support their beliefs. These theists are literally claiming that it's wrong to just assume that others are deluded simply because they have experiences different than yours and then claiming that other people who have experiences different from them must be deluded.

I think this is why, by the way, so many theists focus all their attacks on atheists and not on other theists of different faiths than theirs. They can attack atheists for "believing in something without evidence" and claim that they themselves are far more rational because they have evidence for their beliefs. But when it comes to theists of other faiths, they have to deal with the fact that other theists claim to have the same exact sort of evidence that they do and yet, somehow, have different (and often wholly incompatible) beliefs. Which would just prove that such "evidence" is completely and utterly worthless when it comes to actually providing knowledge or establishing truth (which is exactly what we atheists have been saying all along).

An Incredibly Low Bar for Belief in God

Let me state up front that there are certainly some theists out there who claim to have really good reasons for believing in God. They have, perhaps, examined all the evidence and arguments for and against and have come to what they feel is a rational conclusion that God (specifically the God of the particular religion they belong to, that is) actually exists. Or perhaps they have had a personal spiritual experience of such overwhelming power that they just know with every fiber of their being that God (specifically the God of the particular religion they belong to, that is) exists.

Yes, I am quite sure that there are theists like that out there. You wouldn't know it, though, from the questions and comments theists often post in online forums in an attempt to attack atheists and/or defend their own beliefs. Time and time again, for example, we see theists asking questions such as the following:

Atheists, what evidence (not lack of) do you have that a god cannot possibly exist?

- "How can someone be an atheist, if there is a chance there is a god? Because you can't prove there isn't, then when he dies he will find out he is doomed for eternity."

- "Do atheists actually believe they can prove there is no God?"

- "Has science proven that God does not exist?"

- "Can an atheist prove that there is no creator and there is no life hereafter?"

And many, many other examples asking how atheists can be absolutely, 100% sure that there can't possibly be any sort of god whatsoever. Or asking what scientific evidence atheists can point to in order to justify their assertion that God can't possibly exist. Or asking how someone can be an atheist, if there is a *chance* there might be a god?

Seriously?

Aside from the fact that most atheists do not actually assert that God cannot possibly exist or that they are 100% convinced that God doesn't, in fact, exist, is that really the best justification these theists can come up with to support their belief? Rather than actually trying to present evidence that would support a belief in God or present logical arguments that would show that God likely exists, we atheists are tasked with proving with 100% certainty that no sort of god could possibly exist. Which means, what? That theists are willing to give their belief and commit their lives to something that only "might possibly exist" or that "cannot be conclusively proved with 100% certainty to *not* exist"?

Why is this even a thing? Are we really expected to go through our lives affirmatively believing in anything anybody claims, just because those claims cannot be completely and absolutely proven false with 100% certainty? I can't prove with 100% certainty that reptiloid aliens *aren't* surreptitiously taking the place of world leaders and celebrities in a prelude to global conquest, so that's a reason to believe they are? I can't prove with 100% certainty that the Nigerian prince who is willing to pay me $10 million to help him move currency out of his country (for a small fee upfront) *isn't* a total scam, so I should just fork over my hard-earned money to every single Nigerian prince that sends me an e-mail?

Have theists really set such a low bar for everything they are willing to believe in, or is it limited just to religion? And if it's limited just to religion because, say, the stakes are higher and it's better to believe and be safe than not believe and be sorry (see Pascal's Wager on p. 131), why won't theists apply this same logic to every other religious belief other than their own? I mean, can a Christian, say, really prove with 100% certainty that there's no possibility whatsoever that Islam isn't true? Or can a Muslim really prove with 100% certainty that there's no possibility that Hinduism isn't true? Why such a low bar for their particular religious beliefs but not for everybody else's?

No, atheists cannot absolutely prove with 100% certainty that no sort of "god" can possibly exist. But why on earth would anybody believe in something just because there is a slight — perhaps infinitesimally small — chance that it *might* possibly exist in some form?

What Would Theists Accept as Proof that God Doesn't Exist?

I have previously discussed (see <u>False Equivalency and the Burden of Proof</u> on p. 31) the way that some theists keep trying to shift their burden of proof onto atheists, demanding that atheists "prove" that God *doesn't* exist instead of offering any credible evidence or arguments for their assertion that God *does* exist. As if "you can't prove it doesn't exist" were some sort of rational justification for believing in, well, anything.

On a *seemingly* unrelated note, I have noticed that one of the most popular questions that theists love to ask atheists in various online forums is what it would take to convince an atheist to believe in God or what would atheists accept as proof of the existence of God. Now, I can't say for sure why so many of these questions keep being asked. Perhaps theists expect atheists to be so dead set in their "atheist beliefs" that no amount of proof would ever satisfy them (which would then provide rhetorical ammunition to theists who want to claim that atheists have "blind faith" or are otherwise irrational in their "atheist beliefs.")

Regardless of why these questions get asked, however, they tend to actually get a **lot** of responses from atheists who are only too happy to specify exactly what would convince them. For some, it's as simple as seeing a single amputee regrow a limb after praying for it to happen. For others, it would require that the various promises made in the Bible to the faithful be consistently fulfilled instead of constantly being told that "God moves in mysterious ways" or "God promised to *answer* prayers, but sometimes the answer is *no.*" Some hard-core atheist would require a demonstration of universe creation, since that is the only thing that would definitively distinguish God from, say, an advanced alien race. But regardless of the type of proof that would be expected by various atheists, you don't tend to see atheists just claim that it would be impossible to ever prove the existence of God and therefore nothing you say will ever change my mind LA LA LA LA LA I AM NOT LISTENING!!!

And yet, what happens when a *theist* is asked what could possibly convince them that God *doesn't* exist? What proof would they accept for the *non*-existence of God? Would it be, say, a demonstration that that many prayers of the faithful go unfulfilled? Or perhaps the existence of evil in the world (including natural disasters)? What about evidence that definitively shows that the events described in various holy books never actually took place?

crickets

No, when faced with questions like these, some theists state that NOTHING could ever convince them that God doesn't exist because they know deep in their heart with every fiber of their being that God does, in fact, exist. Their faith is not contingent on things like evidence or rational arguments. They know because they know because they know.

Other theists, however, take an entirely different tack (and I suspect these are the type of theists who ask atheists what would convince them to believe in the first place). When asked what would they accept as proof of the non-existence of God, they suddenly claim that no such proof is possible because it's actually impossible to prove or disprove the existence of God and therefore nothing you say will ever change my mind LA LA LA LA LA I AM NOT LISTENING!!!

Hmmmmm…

And this is where it all comes back to the original discussion regarding the shifting of the burden of proof that theists love to engage in. Seriously, if theists honestly and truly don't believe it is possible to prove or disprove the existence of God and are not just trying to weasel out of their burden of proof yet again, why would they expect atheists to be able to tell them what *they* would accept as proof of God's existence? And if theists *don't* actually believe it's impossible to prove or disprove the existence of God, then please, by all means, they should be willing to tell us what would constitute proof in their eyes for the non-existence of God. Come on, fair is fair. If they're going to demand that atheists "prove" that God doesn't exist, they should at least be willing to first tell us what they would actually consider to be sufficient proof.

The Evidence for the Non-Existence of God

As mentioned in the previous essay, theists who keep asking atheists to provide proof that God *doesn't* exist rarely expect to get an answer and have made it clear that they don't think that any answer is actually possible. The part that annoys me the most about this sort of question, however, is not the fact that they are blatantly obvious attempts to shift the burden of proof from the person making the claim ("God exists") to the person expressing disbelief in that claim. No, what *really* annoys me about these questions is the assumption (stated or unstated) that a lack of expected evidence is somehow not sufficient to establish the non-existence of something and that in order for a claim of non-existence to be justified there must be some sort of independent evidence for that thing's lack of existence. And the reason this annoys me so much is because (a) this same standard is not typically required by anybody when it comes to anything apart from God and (b) **IT MAKE NO SENSE WHATSOEVER!!!**

SIGH

If I say I have an elephant in my garage and demand you prove that this elephant doesn't exist, you can look in my garage and observe that there is no evidence whatsoever of that elephant. No large gray beast in sight, no distinctly elephant-y smell, no pile of hay or mounds of excrement, nothing. Presumably, this would be sufficient evidence to you that the elephant I claim is currently residing in my garage does not, in fact, exist, would it not? And would it matter if I said that a lack of evidence for the elephant's existence doesn't count and that you must instead provide some other independent, positive evidence for the non-existence of my elephant? Of course not, because **THAT MAKES NO SENSE WHATSOEVER!!!**

If I say that an evil race of shape-shifting reptilian aliens are replacing celebrities and world leaders in a prelude to invading our world, the fact that I have zero credible evidence to back up my claim would make you feel justified in not believing me, don't you think? And would it matter if I said that a lack of evidence for the existence of these shape-shifting reptilian aliens doesn't count and that you must instead provide some other independent, positive evidence for the non-existence of these aliens and their nefarious plot to conquer the world? Of course not, because **THAT MAKES NO SENSE WHATSOEVER!!!**

For that matter, a hole in the ground is all the evidence anybody needs in order to believe that the dirt that used to be in that hole is no longer there. A hole is a "lack of evidence" for dirt and there's no way to have any other sort of "positive" evidence for the absence of dirt other than that hole. Looking at a hole and demanding that somebody provide additional evidence that there is no dirt in the hole **MAKES NO SENSE WHATSOEVER!!!**

Take any claim for which we should expect there to be some evidence to support it. Any claim at all. Whether it be elephants in the garage, aliens in the White House, the efficacy of homeopathic remedies, a promise by somebody who says he is a Nigerian prince that he will pay you millions of dollars if you will give him some money up front, or that there exists an intelligent being composed of "pure spirit" (whatever the heck that means) which exists outside of time and space (whatever the heck that means) while somehow still being capable of interacting with the material world and which purportedly cares deeply about every individual member of one particular species living on one particular world orbiting one particular star among billions in one particular galaxy among countless trillions of similar galaxies in this entire vast universe, it doesn't matter. If there is no evidence to support that claim when there s*hould* be such evidence[1], then that is all the evidence that is required to justify a lack of belief in that claim and asking for additional evidence that the thing in question doesn't exist **MAKES NO SENSE WHATSOEVER!!!**

Now, reasonable people can certainly disagree on what actually constitutes "evidence" of God in the first place. While some theists are more than happy to acknowledge the lack of any evidence (since, supposedly, the most important thing in life is to have "faith"), other theists insist that the evidence of God's existence is all around us in the beauty of sunsets and rainbows, in the apparent orderly design of nature, in our DNA and our consciousness (not to mention things like anecdotal stories of miracles, the very existence of various holy books and the supposed truths contained therein, etc.). And atheists, of course, just point out that none of those supposed evidence for the existence of God are actually "evidence" in the first

---

[1] I know that one favorite tactic theists use when atheists point out that there is no evidence for the existence of any gods is to claim that God is some sort of amorphous, undetectable, ineffable, and wholly unknowable and incomprehensible being that exists outside of time and space and the very laws of this universe, and therefore there really s*houldn't* be any sort of evidence for God's existence. If this were actually the case, however, there would be no way for these very same theists to also claim to know what their god is like in the first place, let alone what their god has said and done and promised to do, what their god wants *us* to do (and not do) with our lives, what their god has in store for us in the afterlife, etc. You don't get to claim to worship a god who has said and done and promised to do very specific things and then, when asked to provide any evidence of that god, suddenly claim that it's impossible to know anything about that god.

place since they are either not reproducible, not verifiable and/or nothing more than arguments from ignorance ("You can't explain it so it *must* be due to the particular God I happen to worship!") As a result, it is possible to have a meaningful debate on whether there actually is evidence for God's existence or not. But when somebody argues that there is no evidence for the existence of God, demanding that this person somehow provide independent evidence for the non-existence of God —

[Say it with me now...]

MAKES NO SENSE WHATSOEVER!!!

Detecting the Undetectable God

Quite often, when theists are asked to provide any solid evidence for the god they were most likely indoctrinated from a young age to believe in, they respond by claiming that their god's nature as a "supernatural" being who exists "outside of time and space" makes it wholly and utterly undetectable in any way. Which means, of course, that it's actually *atheists* who are irrational for expecting there to be evidence of such a being and not *theists* for believing in such a being despite a lack of evidence, right?

Not *quite*.

You see, the moment somebody claims to believe in an "undetectable" god of some sort, it necessarily raises the question of how they (or anybody else such as ancient prophets who were inspired to write holy scriptures) can claim to have any knowledge whatsoever about a god that is undetectable, and that is a vexing question indeed! Or, at least, it *would* be a vexing question if they were at all consistent about the god they claim to believe in. Because, you see, the theists who claim that God is "undetectable" (as well as mysterious, unknowable and otherwise "ineffable") are often the same ones who are perfectly happy to tell you everything they know about this completely unknowable god, including what it is like, what it has said and done and promised to do, what it wants us to do (and not do) with our lives, etc. It's only when one of those darned atheists ask them to provide a shred of objective evidence to *support* those claims that the god in question suddenly (and retroactively, of course) becomes "undetectable" in order to explain why no evidence will be forthcoming. Ever.

Now, some theists don't play this game and instead just say that their god *is* detectable and that we can see evidence of his existence all around us. Everything we see around us is, according to them, proof of their god's existence (by definition, if for no other rational reason). Want proof of the things their god is described as doing in their particular holy book? Not a problem! Did you know that (despite what every single qualified geologist might have to say on the subject) the Grand Canyon was obviously carved out in a matter of minutes during the great flood? How about this fossilized dinosaur footprint that appears to be intersected by a vaguely humanoid footprint that clearly proves that humans and dinosaurs coexisted just like it implies in the Bible? Yep, if you squint really hard and are willing to ignore all the evidence that contradicts your beliefs, it's easy to find proof of god's existence all over the place.

But those theists who do play the "undetectable" card really do run into some serious problems even if they refuse to face them. If they truly think that their god is wholly incapable of being detected in any way, then they logically can't claim that they (or anybody else) can know anything whatsoever about this god. An undetectable god cannot speak to prophets, cannot inspire (or write) scriptures, cannot perform miracles, cannot make its presence known in any way, since to do any of that would mean that it was detectable after all. That might work for deists who claim to believe in an utterly useless concept of a "hidden" god who does not interact with the universe at all, but it's a massive problem for anybody who believes in any of the gods actually worshiped throughout all of human history.

When faced with this conundrum, many of these theists then backpedal a bit and say that their god is undetectable *to science*, but still somehow detectable to humans (which might include modern day humans or else just be limited to those humans who lived thousands of years ago and were inspired to write the holy scriptures describing whichever god is being discussed). Which sounds like a pretty reasonable (if suspiciously convenient) way out of this conundrum, right?

Welllllll… not really, sorry.

See, you need to keep in mind is that all of our senses, whether sight or hearing or smell or taste or touch, work according to well-understood (and perfectly detectable) scientific principles. When we see something, it's because a photon has impacted our optic nerve. When we hear something, it's because a sound wave has traveled through the air and vibrated against our ear drum. When we smell something, it's because a scent molecule has come into contact with a scent receptor in our nose. You get the picture. And the point being that we really don't have any physical way to detect anything in some way that couldn't also be detected by a properly calibrated scientific instrument.

But that's OK, since theists have a way out of *that* conundrum as well. Our brains (or, perhaps, our minds or "spirits" or "souls," whatever that actually means) actually have a special ability to detect gods that is not tied to any of our senses. We humans can (or, at least, *could*, sometime in the distant past) hear the voice of god speaking directly to our minds/brains/spirits/souls in a way that does not involve any physical interaction whatsoever and is thus wholly undetectable by scientific instruments. Problem solved, right?

Sure, why not.

Just one *teensy-weensy* little problem, however…

You see, if this special ability to detect the voice of god within us were actually any sort of reliable way to obtain knowledge, then **every single person who claimed to have received such personal revelation would have an equally valid claim that what he or she heard was the truth**. And that would mean that every single religion that claims to be based on revealed truth from god would be equally true and every single prophet who has claimed to have heard from god would equally be telling the truth about what they experienced. Not just the ancient prophets in the Bible, but also Mohammad, Joseph Smith, David Koresh, Hindu mystics of all stripes, and all the rest. And this is especially a problem if you happen to believe in the sort of god who is omnipotent, omniscient and actually *wants* people to know what he says.

Either personal spiritual experiences *are* a valid way of obtaining knowledge about gods (in which case all religions and all prophets are equally true, which cannot be the case due to how different their doctrines are) or else personal spiritual experiences are *not* a valid way of obtaining knowledge about gods (in which case we are right back to the original question as to how theists can actually know anything about their god in the first place).

God Could Provide Evidence of His Existence…

… but He doesn't, since that would somehow take away our Free Will™ (despite the fact that the Bible describes multiple instances where God revealed Himself to people who somehow managed to disobey Him anyway).

Except, of course, that God *does*, in fact, provide all sorts of evidence — tons and tons of evidence — to prove that He exists.

It's just that He's very, very careful to make all the evidence either very unreliable or look like it could have some other explanation, because if He made the evidence indisputable then it would, once again, somehow take away our Free Will™.

Unless, of course, somebody already believes that God exists, in which case all the evidence of His existence really *is* indisputable and just so darn *obvious* to anybody who will just open their hearts and consider it.[2] Because, I guess, if you have already made up your mind to believe in God in advance (especially if you have been indoctrinated from a young age to believe in Him), then God providing you with evidence that He exists *won't* take away your Free Will™ after all.

Which is why, of course, "faith" is defined as both "a strong, unshakeable belief in something despite a lack of evidence to support that belief" and "a strong, unshakeable belief in something because of the strong evidence that supports that belief." It's like a complete misunderstanding of Schrödinger's famous thought experiment where the true state of the evidence supporting a belief in God wholly depends on the frame of mind of the person observing it.

So, to sum up… God will *not* provide indisputable evidence of existence, except that He *will*, and when He does, He will make it look like it's *not* actually indisputable evidence, unless you already believe He exists, in which case it *will* look like indisputable evidence.

[The preceding logic was brought to you by the same people who claim to be able to detect an "undetectable" God and to know everything a supposedly "unknowable" God has said and done and promised to do and wants us to do and not do with our lives.]

---

[2] Confirmation Bias? Never heard of it.

A God-Shaped Hole

Hardly a day goes by when somebody doesn't ask a variation of the same exact question (which I'm sure they think is the perfect "gotcha" question against atheists that nobody else has ever been clever enough to think of):

"What evidence do atheists have that God doesn't exist?"

"Can atheists prove that God doesn't exist?"

"Aren't atheists irrational for believing God doesn't exist when they have no evidence that God doesn't exist?"

"What proof do atheists have to prove there is no God?"

"If God doesn't exist, why is there no proof he doesn't?"

Etcetera, etcetera, *ad infinitum* and *ad nauseam*.

Now, let's ignore for the moment that this is all just an attempt to shift the burden of proof onto atheists in a sad, desperate attempt to hide the fact that these theists have no evidence or proof to support their own beliefs.

And for now, let's also just ignore the oft-quoted aphorisms that "it's impossible to prove a negative" (which only applies to a *universal* negative and not a *specific* negative) and "absence of evidence is not evidence of absence" (which doesn't apply when evidence of something *should* be discoverable if the thing in question actually existed). And the *reason* we can ignore those aphorisms is because, despite the fact that these theists will typically attempt to move the goalposts and claim that "God" is some sort of immaterial, undetectable, mysterious and unknowable "pure spirit" that exists "outside of time and space" and therefore it's impossible to for there to be any evidence of its existence, the reality is that these very same theists claim to worship a very specific deity who they claim has said and done and promised to do very specific things for which, yes, there should be evidence if true. Not all theists, mind you, but definitely the ones who ask questions like this.

So, given the fact that we are talking about a *specific* deity for which there *should* be discoverable evidence if it existed and ignoring just how pathetic it is that the best justification these theists can apparently come up with for their belief is that "nobody can prove that God *doesn't* exist," allow me to present the following analogy:

Let's say you are planning to put an in-ground swimming pool in your backyard. The first step, of course, is to remove all the dirt and grass from the area where you want the pool to go. Once that is done, you now have a hole in your backyard of very specific dimensions. But what, actually, is a hole? It doesn't really exist on its own and isn't something you can see or touch in any way. Instead, it is merely the absence of the dirt and grass that *should* be there under normal circumstances. And yet, we still can know for certain that there is a hole there.

Now, what if you tell your neighbor that you are planning to put an in-ground swimming pool in your backyard and he looks over the fence and asks why you haven't dug a hole for it yet? You, of course, point out that the hole is right there in plain sight for all to see, but he claims that all he can see is an absence of any evidence of dirt and grass and that "absence of evidence is not evidence of absence." And when you point out that a hole is just a matter of there being no dirt or grass in a specified location, he informs you that you still haven't demonstrated the existence of the hole because, as we all know, "it's impossible to prove a negative."

Now, some people talk about having a "God-shaped hole" in their heart, meaning that there is something missing in their lives that they think only a belief in God can fill. But the reality is that there is a God-shaped hole in the universe. Just as the pool-shaped hole for your backyard pool "exists" because a very specific amount of dirt and grass is missing, so, too, does this God-shaped hole "exist" because all the things that *should* be discoverable if God actually existed are missing as well. Just as there is a hole where the dirt and grass in your backyard should be, there is a hole where the evidence of God's existence should be. And there is no need to "prove" the existence of a hole beyond pointing out the absence of what should be there if there weren't a hole.

Seriously, it's not that hard.

Chapter 5.   Why the word "Supernatural" Is Meaningless

Periodically, theists will ask whether atheists reject the entire idea of "the supernatural" all together or whether it's just God (or gods) that we don't believe in. Now, atheists, as a rule, don't claim to have beliefs or knowledge about ultimate or absolute truths (that's usually the realm of theists, and atheists generally say they don't believe those claims). However, speaking just for myself, as far as I am concerned the entire idea of "supernatural" is a wholly empty and meaningless concept to begin with. Sure, it has a dictionary definition, but in my experience "supernatural" is just a term that people use to describe proposed things for which there is no proof or good evidence but which they nevertheless think might *possibly* exist in some sense. Or, perhaps, things that they really *wish* existed despite all evidence to the contrary.

For example:

- We have no real proof or good evidence that God exists, but we really, really wish He did, so let's say that God is "supernatural" to explain why we can't detect any evidence of His existence rather than acknowledging He doesn't actually exist.

- We have no real proof or good evidence that ghosts exist, but we really, really wish they did, so let's say that ghosts are "supernatural" to explain why we can't detect any evidence of their existence rather than acknowledging they don't actually exist.

- We have no real proof or good evidence that psychic powers exist, but we really, really wish they did, so let's say that psychic powers are "supernatural" to explain why we can't detect any evidence of their existence rather than acknowledging they don't actually exist.

- We have no real proof or good evidence that the human spirit or soul exists apart from human brains, but we really, really wish they did, so let's say spirits and souls are "supernatural" to explain why we can't detect any evidence of their existence rather than acknowledging they don't actually exist.

Rinse and repeat.

Now, of course there are things in the world that people can't currently explain. Perhaps there are even things that we will *never* be able to explain (why *does* seeing a person yawn make us want to yawn as well?). But anything that we can **observe** or **detect** or that has any **effect** whatsoever on the natural world is, as far as I'm concerned, **part** of the natural world and therefore, by definition, not supernatural. Or, to put it another way, the supernatural cannot exist because **existence itself is a natural state**.

If I were to try and make a formal logical argument regarding the supernatural, it would look something like the following:

1. Something can be said to exist if it is composed of matter or energy and occupies time and space.

2. Anything that is composed of matter or energy and occupies time and space is part of the natural world.

3. Anything "supernatural" would, by definition, **not** be part of the natural world and would therefore need to not be composed of matter or energy nor occupy time or space.

4. Therefore, anything supernatural cannot be said to actually exist. Q.E.D.

Chapter 6.   Why Do So Many People Believe in [a] God?

One argument I hear periodically is that, even if you can refute the claims of one particular religion, doesn't the fact that almost all cultures throughout human history have held a belief in *some* sort of god or gods mean something? Couldn't this be evidence that there is, in fact, some sort of supernatural creative force "out there" and we all just perceive and interpret it in different ways? If you want to get all scientific (and I always love when people invoke science to justify their non-scientific beliefs), doesn't it show that humans have evolved to believe in God and that it would only make sense if there were, in fact, a God to believe in?

Now, the easiest answer would, of course, be that it doesn't matter if a billion people believe something to be true if the thing is actually false, and humanity has collectively believed a *lot* of wrong ideas throughout history. For untold thousands of years, people believed ("knew") that the sun went around the earth once a day, despite the fact that the earth actually rotates. People believed that illnesses were caused by all matter of things (bad air, curses, etc.), despite the fact that they are actually caused by germs. So yes, most cultures throughout recorded history have believed in some sort of supernatural creator, but (skipping the obvious problem that no two cultures could agree on what that creator actually was like) that doesn't really provide evidence that those beliefs are correct.

Having said that, however, I think the question does deserve a little more nuanced answer. It's not enough to point out that people believe a lot of wrong things, since that doesn't mean that *this* particular belief is wrong (only that it *could* be wrong despite the fact that so many people have held it, or some form of it). Instead, it would be helpful to provide an alternate explanation for why a belief in god or gods seems to be such an ingrained part of human nature. Now, I'm not saying that I can conclusively provide the actual explanation, but I do at least have some thoughts as to one *possible* alternate explanation. Someday I'll write a book on this subject and fill it with annotated footnotes to scientific studies and research, but for now I'm just going to go with a summation of things I have heard and read about, as well as my interpretation of what it all means.

Humans may not have evolved specifically to believe in God, but I think it's safe to say that our intellect and capacity to solve problems certainly evolved as a survival mechanism. Rather than developing armored hides to protect ourselves from danger or razor-sharp claws to bring down prey, humans evolved the ability to anticipate danger to protect ourselves and to solve complex problems in order to figure out ways to obtain food. When early man saw the tall grass swaying, especially in the absence of any evident wind, he realized it could still be caused by the wind but could also be caused by a predator stalking him. If he assumed it was a predator and ran away, he lived to survive another day even if it really was the wind. On, the other hand, if he assumed it was just the wind and it turned out to be a predator, well, he likely wouldn't live long enough to pass his genes to the next generation. And thus, we evolved to see patterns even when they don't exist and to assume agency (*i.e.*, that things are caused by mindful creatures) even when things happen by random chance.

Although this tendency to see patterns and assume agency was instrumental in allowing humans to survive and flourish throughout the millennia, it also brought along some baggage with it. That's evolution for you. Evolution allows species to adapt to changing environments and survive, but there's no guiding force to ensure that a particular adaptation is the "best" possible solution, only that it was better than other adaptations that did not enable a species to survive. This is why we have eyes with built-in blind spots, appendices that serve no purpose and occasionally kill us by bursting and, sad to say, an intellect that assumes that every little bump in the night must be caused by some creature coming to eat us.

The problem is, of course, that our pattern-recognition skills are flawed. Sure, they are good enough to help us survive, but they have also led us to see patterns where they don't exist and also ignore any evidence that contradicts the patterns we have convinced ourselves do exist. If we, for example, see evidence of agency all around us, in the apparent design of the complex natural world or in stories of people being blessed after praying to one God or another, we are going to stick with our beliefs in those patterns even if the apparent natural design can be shown to have an alternate explanation or we hear stories about people who prayed and weren't blessed. Psychologists call this "Confirmation Bias" and it simply means that, once we have made up our minds about something, we tend to accept any evidence supporting that belief and disregard (or ignore) any evidence that contradicts that belief. And again, as a rough survival tool, confirmation bias served us well in the past. The fact that 9 times out of 10 the swaying grass ended up just being caused by the wind doesn't matter if that 10th time ends up being a hungry predator, so it's better to just ignore the cases that don't fit the pattern and see the one case in your favor as proof that swaying grass means death is waiting to attack with sharp, nasty claws and fangs.

So, yeah. Throughout history, human societies have tended to believe in one sort of supernatural force or another. We don't know what that bright yellow thing in the sky is, but it moves and therefore must either be intelligent or else be pulled by something intelligent. And when it hides for most of the day and things get cold, it must be because it is angry with us. So we'd better pray to it and sacrifice things to it just in case. And, sure enough, after a few months of prayers and sacrifices, winter comes to an end and spring returns proving we were right. Except, we now know all about the rotation of the earth, the tilt of its axis and its yearly journey around the sun.

Does the fact that humans, in their ignorance, used to think the sun was a god and worshiped it accordingly really say anything about whether there is a god of some sort? Or does it just speak to our ignorance and gullibility?

Chapter 7.   Why Are Theists So Sure that They Know the Truth?

Many theists go beyond simply believing that a god of some sort exists. Instead, they are convinced that the particular God that they worship is the "one true God" and that they know exactly what their God wants them to do. In addition, many theists seem to think that atheism means non-belief in *their* particular God, wholly ignoring all the other people throughout history who have had different beliefs than them. In the following essays I discuss the hypocrisy of thinking that you (and you alone) know what God *really* wants and the implications of the existence of so many different faiths and god beliefs.

The Issue Isn't "Theists vs. Atheists" but "Theists vs. Everybody Else"

In just about every debate regarding the existence of God, the opposing sides are usually **theists** (those who believe in God) and **atheists** (those who do not believe in God). Similarly, in various online discussion forums, theists of all stripes typically post questions directed at "atheists" (or "agnostics," under the mistaken belief, apparently, that an atheist is somebody who claims to know that God doesn't exist while an agnostic merely is unsure). As a result, the issue in question is usually framed in terms of "There is a God" (or, perhaps, "It is rational to believe in God") vs. "There is no God" (or, perhaps, "It is not rational to believe in God").

This presumption that the issue is always (or even primarily) between theists and atheists involve a massive amount of hubris on the part of the theists, however. It requires the theist to assume as an absolute given that *their* particular concept of God, among all the many thousands of concepts of God throughout all of human history (including the many thousands of concepts of God held by religious people of all stripes in the world today) is the *only* concept of God worth discussing. When a Christian asks a question about why atheists don't believe in "God," or when a Muslim or a Hindu sets out to prove the existence of "God," they don't even bother to define the properties of the God they are discussing. For that matter, when a Baptist or a Born Again Christian or a Catholic or member of any other Christian denomination sets out to prove the existence of "God," they never ever acknowledge that their understanding of God may be unique to their particular denomination of Christianity, let alone to Christianity in general. It's always, "I know that [my] God exists, why can't you atheists agree with me?"

This is, of course, why many atheists respond to questions posted by theists by first asking, "Which God?" And this seems to annoy many theists, who just can't seem to grasp the idea that there are billions of other people who have a different understanding of God (or gods) and who are just as sincere in their beliefs. "Obviously," these theists seem to be saying, "all of *those* beliefs are just ignorant superstitions. We're talking about *my* God who, unique in all of human history, just happens to be real." Did I mention the hubris involved in such an assumption? Devout Christians are just as convinced that *their* concept of God is the right one, as devout Jews are convinced that *their* concept of God is the right one, as devout Muslims are convinced that *their* concept of God is the right one, as devout Hindus are convinced that *their* concept of God is the right one, as devout Zoroastrians are convinced that *their* concept of God is the right one, etc., and within each major religion the numerous sects are all equally convinced that *their* concept of God is the right one and that everybody else has got it wrong.

So, yes, it would be nice if theists would specify exactly what sort of "God" they are talking about when asking questions or attempting to make arguments about "God" instead of just assuming that (a) everybody knows what *their* concept of God is and (b) *their* concept of God is the only one worth discussing. And then, rather than framing the debate as a discussion as to whether "there is a God" (the theist side) or "there isn't a God" (the atheist side), the theists should be forced to acknowledge that what they are *really* arguing for is the proposition, "My personal concept of God is the correct one and every other concept of God ever held throughout the entire history of humanity, including the belief that there is no God, is wrong." And then they should be forced to defend *that* proposition instead of just using the same tired "logical" arguments to "prove" the existence of some sort of nebulous "creator" that applies equally well to most of the concepts of God worshiped by various religions.

No, All Theists Do Not Worship the Same God

Despite the fact that there are many thousands of different religions and sects within those religions, each with their own unique take on what, exactly, "God" is and how He acts (or what, exactly, "gods" are and how they act, for the various polytheistic religions out there), time and again I keep seeing people claim that "it's all the same God" or that "all theists worship the same God, even if they call Him by a different name."

Now, growing up as a Christian (a member of the Church of Jesus Christ of Latter-day Saints) and being taught that the Bible was literally true, this claim was pretty much required in order for the religion as a whole to make any sort of sense. After all, the Bible clearly talks about one God who created the Earth and everything else, so there can't possibly be any other gods out there. And, since the Biblical timeline is supposed to trace back to the beginning of human civilization, the only choice is to assume that every other ancient religion (Greek, Roman, Egyptian, Sumerian, etc.) was actually somehow a corruption of this original true faith in the one God of the Bible. Historical and archaeological evidence to the contrary be damned, that's our story and we're sticking with it, since to do otherwise would be to admit that other civilizations talked about completely different "gods" long before the events in the Old

Testament (including the creation of the world) ever took place. OK, so while this view is not actually supportable by evidence, I can understand why people would cling to it.

A completely different claim, however, is often made that the three so-called "Abrahamic" religions (Judaism, Christianity and Islam) all worship the same God, despite the fact that most of the actual devout members of each of those three religions would probably not agree with this claim. All three religions, the argument goes, all have their roots in the Old Testament, each one building upon that basic concept of God and therefore all actually worshiping the same God when you get right down to it. In fact, it is often said, the word "Allah" in Arabic simply means "the God" and this is a reference to the God described in the Bible.

Except… this really doesn't make much sense. Just because all three religions have a concept of God that can be traced to the same root, the interpretations and extra information added on by each religion is so great as to render the resulting concept of God wholly unrecognizable from one religion to the next. Yes, both Christians and Muslims claim to worship the God described in the Old Testament, but they have changed the core definition of that God so much as to produce an entirely different concept of God.

One big is example is the core Christian concept that Jesus Christ is divine (*i.e.*, that Jesus is, in essence, an aspect of God). You can't have Christianity without Christ, and the fact of Jesus's atoning sacrifice is what evidences the divine mercy that is an essential part of God's very nature. Jews, however, will absolutely not accept that Jesus was the literal son of God, let alone that he is actually an intrinsic part of God. The Jewish concept of God simply will not allow God to have a human component, and the idea of an atoning sacrifice to provide salvation to humanity is a foreign concept. As soon as Christians took the Jewish notion of God and added Jesus to that notion, it ceased to be the same God. Similarly, the fact that Muslims do not accept Jesus as divine ("just" another prophet) means that they do not actually worship the same concept or description of God, regardless if they claim that their belief derives from Biblical sources.

[Thought experiment: Take a 2010 Honda Civic coupe. Chop the frame and add some steel to lengthen it. Hack at the body and rework the pillars until you can fit two more doors so it's now a sedan. Remove the 4-cylinder naturally aspirated gasoline engine and replace it a 6-cylinder supercharged diesel engine. Convert it to all-wheel drive. And then remove all the badges and replace them with ones that say "Smith Motors." Now, take this car and put it side-by-side with a brand new 2017 Honda Civic Coupe and try to justify claiming that they are basically the same car. Sure, they can both trace their roots to the same original model and style of car, but are they really still the same?]

So, then, why do people keep insisting that all Abrahamic faiths do, in fact, worship the same God? Well, some of these folks are legitimate scholars of comparative religions and are merely pointing out the historical fact that each later religion *claimed* to be based on the previous ones. But that's not really the same thing as "worshiping the same God," though, is it? Or that each religion has the same understanding of God's essential nature? As far as I can tell, the answer is no, and that's because legitimate religious scholars (many of whom aren't even religious themselves) often don't have an agenda or an axe to grind.

In my experience, however, there is another group of people who make the claim that all Abrahamic faiths worship the same God, however. These are not serious, impartial religious scholars, but instead appear to be deeply religious individuals, usually of the Christian or Islamic persuasion. And their assertion that all Abrahamic faiths worship the same God seems to be a direct response to the issue raised time and again by atheists that, since there are so many different Gods worshiped by so many different religions, the likelihood of any one God being the true God is not very high. "It doesn't matter that there are so many different religions," they will claim, "since they all basically worship the same God." And this appears to be nothing more than an attempt to perpetuate the false "theist vs. atheist" dichotomy I explored earlier.

As long as these believers can argue that all theists are somehow presenting a unified front when it comes to a belief in God, they can ignore the vast differences among the various religious beliefs and avoid needing to justify why their particular God concept is the only one worth talking about or needing to defend their beliefs against, not just atheists, but every other belief system that contradicts theirs.

The Hypocrisy and Hubris of Biblical Interpretation

The following essay deals specifically with the Christian religion and the Bible, since that is what I am most familiar with. Whether it applies to other religions and their holy books — and to what degree — I leave for others to decide.

First, a few premises:

1. Christianity is ultimately based on the Holy Bible. Sure, you can say that Christianity is based on the teachings of Christ, but those teachings can only be found in the Bible. And Christianity (for most Christians, at least) extends well beyond just the words of Christ and encompasses instead all the moral laws and principles found throughout the entire Bible.

2. Christians, on the whole, believe that the Bible's primary purpose is to act as a guideline to show us the path toward

salvation. Only by following the laws and moral principles in the Bible can we learn about Christ, follow his commandments[3] and be saved. So, obviously, it is vitally important to know exactly what the Bible says and what it actually means.

3. Since the time the Bible was first assembled in its current form, some 1700 or so years ago, billions of people have relied on it to show them the path toward salvation.

4. God, according to Christian beliefs, is an omnipotent, omniscient and all-loving father who actually *wants* all of his children (that's us) to learn and follow the path toward salvation. Sure, we are given free will to choose whether to follow the path or not, but the path should be clear and unambiguous enough to follow if we choose to do so.

OK, assuming those premises are more or less accurate, let's move on to the hypocrisy and hubris part.

One trend in modern apologetics ("defending the faith" or, as I like to define it, "attempting to logically justify something that is believed for non-logical reasons," but I digress) is to deal with supposed contradictory, scientifically impossible and/or morally reprehensible passages in the Bible by claiming that one must have special knowledge in order to understand what the passages *really* mean. This takes many different forms, including the following:

• "One must have studied the original languages in which the Bible was written in order to understand what the passage really means."

---

[3] Yes, I am aware that many "Born Again" Christians believe that the *only* thing necessary for salvation is to accept Jesus.

- "One must have a deep understanding of the socioeconomic factors that existed at the time the passage was written in order to understand what it really means."

- "One must fully understand the culture of the people to whom the passage was addressed in order to understand what it really means."

- "One must read the 'forgotten' or 'apocryphal' books of the Bible that were not included at the time it was formally assembled, but really should have been included in order to understand what the passage *really* means."

- Etc., etc., etc.

One common example of this approach is when people try to justify things like the approval of keeping slaves as stated in the Old Testament. "No, no," they will claim, "if you look at the original Hebrew and consider the culture and socioeconomic climate at the time the Old Testament was written, you'll see that this was actually a very *good* kind of slavery and not at all like the slavery you are thinking of!" This, despite the fact that these passages were actually used as *justification* for keeping slaves by Christians in the American South prior to (and, sadly, even after) the Civil War. Gee, what a pity those Christians didn't have access to the original Hebrew version of the Bible. Or know how to read ancient Hebrew even if they did. Or have any way of knowing what the culture and socioeconomic climate was at the time the Old Testament was written…

Which leads me to the whole hypocrisy and hubris angle.

First, the **hypocrisy**. On one hand, these apologists believe that an omniscient, omnipotent and all-loving God would require his children to do certain things in order to gain salvation (and avoid eternal torment) and that the only way to learn what those things are is to read the Bible. But on the other hand, they are asserting that is no way for the vast majority of his children to actually know for sure what the words in the Bible actually mean unless they become Biblical scholars, study ancient dead languages, become experts in anthropology, etc. Especially when you take into account that, for the majority of the history of Christendom, believers were actually *forbidden* to read the Bible (which is why it existed solely in Latin for many centuries). So it is hypocritical to hold people to a standard that they cannot possibly meet while simultaneously claiming that it's all part of a loving God's plan for them.

And then, of course, the **hubris**. Christianity has been practiced in many forms for nigh on two thousand years. Billions of people have been born and died and have failed to understand what the Bible — the one and only guideline toward salvation — actually says. But now, two thousand years later, after all of this, here comes these apologists who are apparently the first and only of all of God's children to finally understand it all. Just because they are so darn special, of course. And smart. Unlike all those poor deluded saps (*i.e.*, 99.999% of humanity) who got it wrong all these years (oh, well, sucks to be them, I guess!)

OK, so maybe I'm overstating things a *wee* bit. But the fact remains that any time an apologist claims that they have some sort of special knowledge or training or insight that allows them to know what a Biblical passage *really* means, in contrast to how the vast majority of Christians have understood that same passage since Christianity began, it is hubris of the highest order. Especially if you think that God actually wanted His children to understand it all along.

The Incomprehensible and/or Imperceptible God

In the previous section I wrote about the hypocrisy and hubris evidenced by people who claim to be the only ones who "really" understand what the Bible actually says. The basic point was that it was incredibly arrogant for anybody to think that (a) God actually wants people to know what He wants people to do and (b) throughout all of human history nobody has been able to figure it out until now (meaning, of course, that billions of people in the past got it all wrong and were presumably doomed to go to Hell as a result).

Well, I have recently run into a similar group of incredibly arrogant theists. They don't claim to just understand the Bible better than anybody else, though. Instead, they claim to understand the *essential nature of God* better than anybody else. God, you see, is wholly incomprehensible to the human mind and therefore *every single religion throughout history* that has ever described God in any particular way just got it wrong.

For example:

> As "God", by the very nature of its defined and understood being, exists outside of the physical Universe, there will be no exclusively applicable, scientifically validated or accepted physical or empirical "evidence" of the existence of God.

Or these gems:

> God is an inner experience that no words can explain. The one Creator God created all other gods (small "g") including the ones you named. None are equal to the Creator God who created them.

> The truth of God can be known only by reaching beyond the relativity of the material realm consciousness. It is an inner experience perceived when the human's consciousness is raised to its higher mind. Those who meditate know of the higher mind.

There are no outer writings or teachings that can explain God for the conscious mind of the human and no religion is necessary for the inner experience of God. When the human is ready the teacher will appear. That teacher is the inner experience of God.

Now, as I mentioned, this *appears* to be just another example of people who are so full of themselves, who think they are so special, that they honestly believe that they are among the select few in the history of religion to truly understand who and what God "really" is. I'm sure it makes them feel good about themselves, but what type of person can believe in a God who actually cares about us and then thinks that billions of humans throughout history just got it wrong?

However, I think there may be more to it than just sheer arrogance. I suspect that at least part of this has to do with an acknowledgement that there really is no valid evidence to support a belief in the existence of God. And rather than just admit this, these people have decided to redefine God in a way that does not require any evidence. As with the deist notion of a non-interventionist God, however, what's left is an empty meaningless concept of a god who doesn't perform miracles, doesn't promise an afterlife or salvation, doesn't provide moral guidance, etc. It's just yet another cop-out to justify why they can't provide any evidence for God's existence.

Of course, one question that never seems to get fully addressed is how, if God is so incomprehensible, do people like this seem to know so much about Him in the first place, including what He wants us to do, what He can do for us, etc. Now that's the real mystery! After all, if you're actually talking about one of the many, many gods actually worshiped by anybody throughout all of recorded human history, these gods have not exactly been shy about showing themselves (or allowing themselves to be perceived, if you prefer) in the past, at least if you believe all the various accounts in the various holy books that provide the only source of knowledge that believers actually have regarding their gods. So it's rather disingenuous to claim that the particular "God" you worship created the universe, performed a multitude of miracles, talked to various people, sent down representatives to interact with humans, made specific promises, provided moral guidelines for us to follow, etc., etc., etc., and then go on to claim that this "God" cannot be perceived in any way.

Is God's Will Simple to Understand?

A common assertion from theists is that God's will is simple to understand by anybody who will actually take the time to seek to learn it. And so, I figured I would take this claim and see where it leads (in a slightly tongue-in-cheek manner, of course).

Of *course* God's will is simple to understand! After all, He loves all of us and really wants us all to know His will so we can return to Heaven and worship Him for all eternity, right? What sort of monster would require us to know His will in order to avoid eternal torment and then *not* make it simple to understand His will?

Anyway, here are the six easy steps to know God's will in all things:

1. First of all, you just need to decide which of all the many gods worshiped throughout human history is the **one true God** in the first place. Zeus? Odin? Amun-Ra? Marduk? Quetzalcoatl? Ba'al? Amaterasu-Ōmikami? Tāne? Vishnu? Ahura Mazda? Jehovah (a.k.a. Allah)? Each God has different attributes and offers a different path to salvation (not to mention has different holy books written about Him/Her/It), so it's vitally important you select the right one. OK, so it's probably not one of the Gods

worshiped by ancient civilizations[4], but at the very least you will need to pick between the God of the so-called "Abrahamic" religions (Judaism, Christianity and Islam), the God of Hinduism, the God of Zoroastrianism, the God of Sikhism, etc. Still, it's probably whichever God your parents just so happen to believe in[5], so that's easy enough.

2. Then, once you've figured out which is the one true God, decide which of the various **religions** worshiping that God is the one true faith in that God. If you've opted for, say, Jehovah/Allah, then you would simply need to decide whether Judaism, Christianity or Islam is the **one true faith**. Each main religion has very different ideas of what their chosen God wants us to do, so once again it's vitally important to pick the right religion. After all, what if you pick Judaism and it turns out that the bit about Christ was true after all? Or what if you pick Christianity and it turns out that Muhammad actually was God's final prophet? What if you dutifully pray toward Mecca five times each day and it turns out that God really wanted you to observe the Sabbath once a week instead? Again, though, it's probably whichever God your parents happened to believe in, right? Lucky you for being born into the right family and the right culture and the right country, eh? Pity about everybody else who wasn't so lucky, but what can you do?

3. Next, once you've figured out which is the correct religion, decide which of the many, many **denominations** of that religion is the correct one. If, say, you picked Christianity as the one true faith, just figure whether the correct denomination is Catholics, Episcopalians, Latter-day Saints (a.k.a. Mormonism), Baptists,

---

[4] We all know what a bunch of ignorant and superstitious people those ancients all were, am I right?
[5] What an amazing coincidence!

Born Again Christians, Seventh-day Adventists, Pentecostals, Methodists, Shakers, Quakers, Lutherans, Calvinists, Anabaptists, Greek Orthodox, Russian Orthodox, Church of Christ, etc. Keep in mind that each denomination interprets the holy scriptures in a different way, and one denomination's "salvation comes by grace alone" is another denomination's "faith without works is dead." A little harder here, since people do tend to convert from one denomination to another and you may not be able to rely on the denomination your parents belonged to. But, still — it can't be that hard to know which one is the right one, can it? No pressure, though — it's not like the fate of your everlasting soul depends on it or anything[6].

4. OK, now that you've figured out which is the correct denomination of the correct religion of the correct God, you may also need to decide which particular **sect** of that denomination really knows what God's will is. For example, if you selected Baptist as the correct denomination of the correct religion of the correct God, you will now have to decide whether the correct sect is Southern Baptist Convention, National Baptist Convention, Nigerian Baptist Convention, National Missionary Baptist Convention of America, National Baptist Convention of America, Baptist Union of Uganda, Baptist Community of Western Congo, Baptist General Convention of Texas, Baptist Convention of Tanzania, Brazilian Baptist Convention, Progressive National Baptist Convention, Baptist Bible Fellowship International, American Baptist Churches, Lott Carey Foreign Mission Convention, Baptist Community of the Congo River, National Primitive Baptist Convention of the U.S.A., Myanmar Baptist Convention, Cooperative Baptist Fellowship, Baptist General Association of Virginia, Baptist Convention of

---

[6] Oh, wait…

Kenya, Council of Baptist Churches in Northeast India, Nagaland Baptist Church Council, Korea Baptist Convention, Samavesam of Telugu Baptist Churches, Orissa Evangelical Baptist Crusade, National Baptist Convention (Brazil), Church of Christ in Congo–Baptist Community of Congo, Baptist Convention of Malawi, Garo Baptist Convention, Convention of Philippine Baptist Churches, Ghana Baptist Convention, Union of Baptist Churches in Rwanda, American Baptist Association, Baptist Missionary Association of America, Conservative Baptist Association of America, National Association of Free Will Baptists, Convention of Visayas and Mindanao of Southern Baptist Churches, Manipur Baptist Convention or Baptist Community in Central Africa. Again, each sect is bound to interpret the main doctrine of the denomination in a different way unique to their own culture. I know this sounds daunting, but I'm sure if you pray to God and ask Him (or Her or It), She/He/It will be happy to let you know. Just make sure you pray sincerely (just like everybody else) and I'm sure God won't steer you wrong[7].

5. Now that you've selected the correct sect of the correct denomination of the correct religion of the correct God, go pick the **congregation** you think has the most knowledgeable preachers and teachers. After all, the Southern Baptist church down the street may be full of budding heathens and atheists or just ignorant folks who don't really understand the word of God. At this point, you're almost there, so you can be sure that God wouldn't steer you toward the wrong congregation. Just go with

---

[7] Just because God apparently steered wrong everybody who picked a different sect than you doesn't mean He would ever steer **you** wrong. After all — you're special! Billions and billions and billions of people on the earth since the beginning of time and all desperately hoping to know what God's will really is. But they weren't all special like you are, so it's OK.

whichever one makes you feel the most comfortable and be assured that God has directed you (*and you alone, among all the billions of his children, because you are just so danged special[8]*) to the right place.

6. Finally, once you've selected the right congregation of the right sect of the right denomination of the right religion of the right God, all you need to do now is figure out which of the many **preachers and teachers** within that congregation actually understands what the holy book of that religion actually means. Sadly, each individual preacher or teacher will likely have their own interpretation, so it's vitally important that you only listen to the one who has it 100% right. Should you shun homosexuals or welcome them? Should you donate money to homeless people or is that just encouraging bad habits? Do women really need to be subject to their husbands' will or not? Is it enough to just accept Jesus into your heart, or do you actually need to do good deeds and repent for your sins? Is it really harder for a rich man to enter the kingdom of heaven than it is for a camel to pass through the eye of a needle, or is that just a metaphor? Does "turn the other cheek" mean you can't own a gun for self-defense? Did God really just promise to "answer prayers" (and sometimes the answer is "no") or did he actually promise to give "whatsoever we ask for in faith"? Is lusting after a woman in your heart really the same as committing adultery, or was Jesus just being metaphorical again? What's the best way to "love thy neighbor as thyself" while still preventing transgender people from using the bathroom they feel most comfortable in? Is it OK to vote for somebody who claims to share your values if he talks about sexually assaulting women, mocks disabled people and

---

[8] Did I mention just how very special and lucky you are? I mean, just think of the odds! Seriously, you should go out and play the lottery right now.

lies all the time? What, actually, *would* Jesus do? And so on and so forth.

See? Easy as pie!

Chapter 8.   Responses to Arguments for the Existence of God

Although some theists are more than happy to admit that their belief in their particular God is wholly based on faith and they neither need nor offer any evidence whatsoever that their God exists, there are many apologists who do assert that there is abundant evidence that God exists. Or, if not evidence, at least logical arguments that either support a belief in a god of some sort or else outright prove that a god of some sort must necessarily exist. To people untrained in philosophy and logical argumentation, these arguments can seem very powerful on their face, so the following essays provide my responses to various of these arguments.

God of the Gaps

As we discover more and more of the laws of nature and are able to explain how everything in the universe came to be in its current state through purely physical means, where does that leave God? God is necessary, according to most religions, to explain what cannot otherwise be explained. He is a supernatural force that becomes the default explanation for anything we don't understand. Once we understand everything, however, what is the rationale for still believing that the universe needed a God? And if God is not a necessary force, then he is nothing more than a figment of our collective consciousness.

Life was a lot simpler back when we didn't understand anything and it was easy to just posit God (or gods) as the explanation for everything. Why did the sun rise each morning? God did it. Why did it rain yesterday? God did it. Why didn't it rain today? God did it. How did we get here? God did it. Why is there so much pain and suffering in the world? God did, er, well let's just change the subject, shall we? We laugh at ancient cultures who invented gods to explain natural phenomena that we fully understand today. And yet, some still cling to the "god" explanation for the few things that we still don't have good explanations for (or things which they personally don't understand).

As our knowledge of the universe has expanded, however, we've pushed the necessity for God as an explanation into a smaller and smaller box, until he's limited to having started the whole thing in motion in the first place but hasn't really done much since then.

Science has done a wonderful job of explaining just about every facet of creation to the point that "God" is no longer a necessary explanation for anything. We're still a bit fuzzy on how it all got started in the first place (although I don't think modern scientists actually think it all suddenly appeared "OUT OF NOTHING"). At most, that leaves open the possibility that some sort of "god" started the whole process going and then left it to run unassisted. Since there's no actual evidence of such a god apart from our lack of understanding, however, there's really no good reason to assume that such a god actually exists. Any more than there was a good reason to assume the existence of Thor simply because we didn't understand how thunder and lightning happened.

Yes, scientific theories come and go (or get refined over time), and some things that we think we can fully explain today may turn out to have a different explanation later on. But (and this is probably the most important point of all) **even if every single scientific theory ever advanced to explain the universe was completely and utterly wrong, there still wouldn't be a single bit of good evidence to believe in the God of the Bible (or any of the many, many other gods that have been written about over the past thousands of years)**. And there are plenty of Muslims who are just as convinced that Allah, as described in the Koran, is the one true God and not the God of the Bible and they make the same exact arguments as Christians do to justify their belief. They are just as sure, just as convinced, and just as wrong.

Some theists argue that since "science" (or, more properly, the scientific method) does not currently provide an "overarching and all-inclusive" description of reality, we therefore need God to explain what science cannot. To this argument, I offer the following rebuttals:

1. The proper question is not *does* science offer an overarching and all-inclusive description of reality, but whether it *can* offer such a description. Just because we can't explain everything at the moment doesn't mean we won't ever be able to.

2. This is a false dichotomy. Even if science *can't* explain everything about everything, that doesn't mean that religion can (or that it can explain the "gaps" where science fails). Made-up stories by ancient civilizations have no claim whatsoever to any sort of explanatory authority.

In other words, the scientific method is the *only* way we can explain anything about anything. If something can't be explained via the scientific method, it can't be explained, period. Lots of room for ideas, suggestions and general wishful thinking, true, but not actual explanations.

On a related note, one odd question that occasionally gets asked by theists is how one can possibly be an atheist when science hasn't yet (or can't possibly have) explored the entire universe. The presumption being, apparently, that atheists shouldn't be so confident that God doesn't exist when there are distant parts of the universe where, what, God could be hiding? Well, let me just say this about that:

First of all, the majority of atheists don't actually claim to know that God doesn't exist, only that they don't *believe* God exists. This lack of belief could be the result of never being exposed to or raised with a belief in the whole God concept in the first place, it could be a rejection of claims made by theists due to a lack of convincing evidence, or what have you. To be an atheist you don't need to know or claim to know that God doesn't exist, just not believe that God exists. But, hey — there are certainly *some* atheists who are confident enough to say that they have considered the evidence *for* God's existence, as well as the evidence *against* his existence, and are as sure that God doesn't exist as they are sure about anything else in life (*e.g.*, that they are conscious, that the earth rotates and revolves around the sun, that they only have one head, etc.). I should know, since I am one of these atheists.

Second of all, even if you are only talking about atheists like me who claim to "know" that God doesn't exist, the God we are talking about is the exact same God that all the various world religions talk about. You know, the God that actually is described in various holy scriptures, the God that supposedly performs miracles, the God that supposedly provides objective morality, the God that answers prayers, the God that rewards us for following his word and punishes us for not doing so, etc. In other words, the God that — regardless of your religion — actually manifests itself right here where we all happen to live in this incredibly vast, vast universe. Whether or not there is some being that could somehow be described as a "God" in some distant corner of the universe, perhaps even wholly outside the observable universe, that "God" could not possibly be the God that we are talking about here.

A Response to the Argument from Design

The so-called "Argument from Design" is one of the most common and most powerful arguments that theists have at their disposal when they want to argue for the existence of God. It gets trotted out during nearly every debate between theists and atheists, it underpins the entire "Intelligent Design" movement, and is often the sole argument that your average, run-of-the mill theist (as opposed to professional apologists) can think of when asked to justify his or her belief in God. And when I say it is a powerful argument, I simply mean that it is highly persuasive, not that it is actually a particularly sound or valid argument.

In a nutshell, the Argument from Design simply states that the entire observable universe provides evidence that some intelligent being purposely designed it, and this being is what we commonly call "God." A more formal statement of the argument might look similar to the following:

1. Much of what we can observe in the universe has the appearance of being designed.

2. Things that appear to be designed most likely were designed, especially when they are too complicated to have happened any other way.

3. Anything that is designed must, by definition, have a designer.

4. The act of designing requires intelligence and purpose.

5. Therefore, there must be an intelligent and purposeful being or entity who designed the universe, and this is a label that fits our traditional notions of God.

Let me try and tackle these points one at a time.

Much of what we can observe in the universe has the appearance of being designed.

It is certainly true that much of what we can observe in the universe, especially here on Earth, has the appearance of being designed. The key word, of course, being *appearance*. To say that everything we observed actually *is* designed, however, is to assume the very point being argued, so we have to stick with *appears to be designed* at this stage in the argument. We also need to keep in mind that the whole "appears to be designed" thing really doesn't apply to *everything* we observe. Yes, we have learned through centuries of careful scientific observation how cells work like tiny machines and that higher organisms are made up of trillions of cells working together in unison. But much of what we observe beyond our planet has the appearance of sheer chaos.

Things that appear to be designed most likely were designed, especially when they are too complicated to have happened any other way.

This is really the crux of the entire Argument from Design. If something appears to be designed and there's no way for it to have happened other than being designed, it must therefore have been designed. This is the argument made so famously by William Paley some two hundred years ago when he used a pocket watch as an analogy to the natural world. When we encounter something as complex as a pocket watch, the very fact of its existence and complexity testifies to the fact that it was designed by an intelligent creator and did not just occur by chance. Similarly, we can look at the natural world – the complex organisms, the cycle of the seasons, the movement of the stars and planets – and know that it couldn't all have happened by chance.

Another, more modern, analogy compares the natural world to a painting found hanging from a tree in a forest. Only a fool would see that painting, frame and all, and think it possible that it could have just happened by the chance accumulation of elements over time or that it just grew there exactly like that.

The problem with analogies, however, is that they are just that – analogies. They are attempts to explain something by comparing it to something else and are not statements of fact or proofs in and of themselves. As a result, an analogy is only as good as the things being compared. In this case, the watch and painting analogies fail for a number of reasons, including the following:

First, in both analogies, the object in question is found in isolation in a situation where it is clearly different from its surroundings. Nature, on the other hand, is a unified whole.

Second, it's easy to identify a watch or a painting as designed because we have seen numerous other examples of watches and paintings that have all been designed. We know the processes involved in making a watch or painting a picture, so it's safe to assume that any other watch or painting we discover was made in a similar fashion. The same is not true with items in nature, however. We have never seen anybody make a cell or a bear or a tree and therefore can't say that the process must be the same as things made outside of nature.

Third, we can "know" that a watch or a painting is designed because there is no other way to explain how it could come to be. The same used to be true for items in the natural world, but we now have much greater knowledge and can explain how seemingly complex natural items could arise purely by natural processes. And keep in mind that "by natural processes" is not the same thing as "by random chance," since natural processes can include a great degree or organization and direction, even if not driven by any purposeful intelligence (see *Accepting Evolution* on p. 206 for a more in-depth discussion of this).

Finally, any claim that something "couldn't impossibly have occurred unless it was designed" is really just a statement of personal ignorance as to the mechanisms involved. This is often referred to as the problem of "Irreducible Complexity," which sounds scientific, but is really just a made-up term that means "I don't understand how evolution works." It used to be argued, for example, that the human eye was so complex that it had to have been created all at once and couldn't possibly have evolved over time. Recent studies have shown, however, exactly how a complex eye could have evolved over time, starting from light-sensitive cells and eventually becoming the imperfect organs we have today. "But what good is a partial eye," you may ask? Just look at all the creatures alive today that have less evolved eyes and ask them how their "partial eyes" benefit them compared to not having any eyes at all.

Anything that is designed must, by definition, have a designer.

Well, true, I suppose that's purely a matter of definition. If you assume that something is designed, it must have a designer *of some sort*. The problem with this (aside from the fact that it's really just a tautology like saying "anything painted has a painter" or "any thought has a thinker") is two-fold:

First, as discussed above, the mere *appearance* of design doesn't necessarily mean that something was, in fact, designed.

Second, the word "designed" presumes the existence of intelligence and purpose, whereas more neutral terms like "created" or "formed" do not. A falling meteorite can create a crater. Years of dripping water can form marvelous looking stalactites and stalagmites in a cave. Neither of these occurrences involves purpose or intelligence. Unfortunately, some people like to use the term "design" to simply mean "created" or "formed" and thereby claim that some purposeful and intelligent designer must, by definition, have been behind it.

The act of designing requires intelligence and purpose.

This point is really nothing more than anthropomorphism at its worst. Since we design things and we are intelligent and purposeful, we assume that all things that are "designed" must also be done by some entity that is intelligent and purposeful. However, as discussed previously, what many people call "design" is more properly referred to as "creation" or "formation" and these words do not require any sort of intelligence or purpose at all.

Therefore, there must be an intelligent and purposeful being or entity who designed the universe, and this is a label that fits our traditional notions of God.

Well, since I've already addressed the problems with all the underlying premises, there's no further need to show why this conclusion is false. I will point out the leap in logic, however, required to go from "an intelligent being who designed the universe" and "my personal concept of a God." There are many different and contradictory notions of God throughout the world and throughout history, and everybody who uses the Argument from Design seems to use it to justify a belief in a different God. If the Argument from Design works just as well to "prove" the existence of Jehovah as it does Allah, Shiva or Zeus, maybe the argument isn't quite as powerful as it's cracked up to be.

In reality, all the Argument from Design attempts to prove is the existence of some sort of intelligent designer. Sure, it *could* be the particular God of the person making the argument, but why assume so? Heck – given all the observable flaws with the natural world (genetic diseases, blind spots, vestigial organs, etc.), one might argue that the Argument from Design best provides evidence for a malevolent or incompetent god or gods instead of the all-powerful, all-loving Christian God.

A Response to the Cosmological Argument

It is said that there is nothing new under the sun, and that may very well be true. As I watch various apologists try to justify their belief in God (whether it be the God of Christendom, the God of Islam, or some other version of God), most of them at some point fall back on some form of the so-called "Cosmological" argument that has actually been around for quite a long time and has its roots in ancient Greek philosophy (despite the fact that, as far as I am aware, the God that Aristotle was trying to prove was neither the Christian nor the Muslim God).

Some modern apologists go to great lengths to add numerous subtle nuances to the argument to patch its obvious flaws, but the basic formation of the argument has been codified as the "Kalām Cosmological Argument" (KCA) that reads as follows:

1. Everything that begins to exist has a cause

2. The universe began to exist

3. Therefore, the universe has a cause.

On its face, this is a perfectly *valid* argument in the sense that the conclusion logically follows from its premises. There are, however, some serious problems with the argument that basically render it completely useless, as I will discuss in detail in this post.

A Valid Argument Is Not the Same as a Sound Argument

As stated above, a "valid" argument is one which the conclusion logically follows from the stated premises. However, in order to be at all useful, an argument must also be "sound." In order to be sound, the conclusion must not only logically follow from the premises, the premises themselves must also be actually true.

For example, the following is a perfectly *valid* argument that is completely unsound:

1. All elephants can fly

2. Dumbo is an elephant

3. Therefore, Dumbo can fly

This argument is unsound for a variety of reasons, namely that the first premise is **not actually true** and the second premise refers to a fictional character that **doesn't actually exist**. Therefore, this argument is completely useless as an attempt to prove that Dumbo can fly, regardless of whether or not Dumbo really exists and can, in fact, fly. In other words, **an unsound argument doesn't necessarily mean the conclusion is false, but it simply isn't useful in proving that conclusion**.

Another example, perhaps a bit closer to the KCA, would be as follows:

1. All swans have white feathers

2. Black swans are swans

3. Therefore, black swans have white feathers

Again, the problem with this argument is with the first premise. What makes this argument a bit more subtle than the Dumbo example, however, is the fact that most swans *do*, in fact, have white feathers. It's even possible that, before the discovery of the black swan in Australia, *every* species of swan ever encountered did, in fact, have white feathers. But there's a huge difference between saying, "All swans have white feathers" and saying, "All swans **that we are currently aware of** have white feathers." A lack of understanding that empirical evidence is not the same as absolute truth could therefore lead somebody to follow up by claiming that, since black swans must (according to the argument) have white feathers, it must be the case that black swans have a special kind of magical white feathers that just appear black to our eyes instead of just acknowledging that the argument is flawed.

Keeping that in mind, let's take another look at the KCA, but with a few annotations added in:

1. [*Based on our limited empirical experience,*] whatever begins to exist has a cause of its existence.

2. The universe began to exist [*depending on your definition of "universe" and assumed to be true because humans aren't comfortable with the idea of an infinite regress*].

3. Therefore, the universe has a cause [*unless, of course, the universe is a special case of something that began to exist without having a cause, or unless the universe didn't actually have a true beginning as would be the case if it were part of a multi-verse or in an eternal cycle of expansion and contraction*].

The first premise is based on empirical evidence of how things we currently observe behave, but isn't necessarily true for all cases everywhere. Perhaps the universe is the exception to this general rule (after all, we have never observed a universe come into being before, so we can't know whether it follows the same rules as everything else within that universe that we have observed). Perhaps things come into being by themselves all the time, but just not where we can observe it (or where we have yet observed it). Or perhaps the entire premise is just flat out wrong and, as physicist Lawrence Krauss describes in his book, "A Universe from Nothing," particles routinely *do* pop in and out of existence all around us all the time. Either way, there's simply no justification to accept as absolute the premise that whatever begins to exist must have a cause. It may seem to be common sense and may seem to be based on our experience with the natural world, but that doesn't make it necessarily true by any stretch of the imagination.

As an aside, it's interesting to note that early formations of the Cosmological Argument simply had "Everything that exists has a cause of its existence. The big "breakthrough" of the KCA was adding "that begins to exist" to get around the obvious observation that God, as a being who exists, would also necessarily need a cause of his existence. All we have to do then is magically redefine God as a being who never had a beginning (or "exists outside of time and space") and voila! Problem supposedly solved. Except, not really. More on this later...

As for the second premise, the Bible states that God created the universe out of nothing. That's not what science says, however. The Big Bang theory doesn't explain how the universe was created but simply describes the expansion of the known universe from an seemingly infinitely dense and infinitely small singularity that presumably contained within itself all matter and energy. Where did that singularity come from and what caused it to expand? Nobody knows, but there are numerous theories that do not require any sort of intelligent causation.

Now, some modern apologists try to finesse the argument here by claiming that the universe *must* have had a beginning since the concept of an "actual" infinity (as opposed to, I assume, the "virtual" infinities that are used in and even required by various disciplines of mathematics and physics) is "metaphysically" impossible. And by "metaphysically" impossible, these apologists basically mean that the concept makes no sense to them. OK, so maybe I'm oversimplifying their view a *wee* bit, but their arguments against "actual" infinities rely on discussions of logical contradictions such as how an infinite amount divided in half would produce two infinite amounts. And they then claim that this supposed impossibility of an "actual" infinity means that there must have been a beginning to everything at some point, even if you assume the universe is cyclical or budded off from a pre-existing multiverse.

Since the first two premises are not necessarily true, the conclusion is not justified. The premises *could* possibly be true, but there's nothing that *requires* them to be true, and therefore the argument fails on its face as an unsound argument. Again, this doesn't prove that the conclusion is false, only that this argument doesn't prove it to be true.

What if the Conclusion Is True?

OK, so the cosmological argument isn't sound and therefore the conclusion that the universe had a cause isn't *necessarily* true. But it *could* still be true, right? And perhaps, some would argue, it's extremely *probable* even if not *necessarily* true.

So let's go there and assume for the sake of argument that the conclusion *is* actually true and there actually *was* a cause to the universe (either our current universe or the theoretical cyclical universe or multiverse). So what? Even if we accept that the universe somehow had some sort of "cause," we still don't know anything about what that cause was. Could the universe be its own cause (again, we've never observed a universe come into being before, so we can't say what the rules are for universe creation)? Why does it have to be an intelligent being (lots of things happen by random chance, so why do we insist that the creation of the universe must have been done on purpose)?

Some apologists start with the conclusion that the universe must have had a "cause" of some sort and try to make all sorts of inferences as to what this cause must be like. For example, since whatever caused space and time to exist in the first place can't possibly exist in space or time itself, this cause must therefore be somehow timeless (a.k.a "eternal") and immaterial. Gee, they then claim, this sounds an awful like the God of [insert pet religion here], since that God is described as being eternal and a being of pure mind. Except... Well, first of all, there's no explanation given as to how something that is timeless and immaterial could actually have any interaction whatsoever with time and space. It just did. Second of all, God isn't actually described as a "pure mind" in any of the holy scriptures (in fact, he is described as a physical being who interacts with his creations). Third, while God is described as being "eternal" in the holy books, that's not the same as "existing outside of time" or "timeless." It just means he has existed forever and will exist forever, "forever" being a measurement of time and not a state outside of time.

These apologists will also argue that whatever caused the universe to exist must be an "agent" of some sort, meaning an intelligent being. And this is supposedly because something had to *choose* to create the universe or else it would have stayed in its uncreated state forever. And only an intelligent being is capable of choosing. Except... the whole concept of choosing implies the passage of time. The whole concept of a being sitting around saying, "No universe yet, no universe yet, wait for it... NOW!" only makes sense if you're talking about a being that exists within time and not outside of it. Besides, there's no logical requirement that something like the creation of the universe must be the result of choice in the first place. If quantum theory teaches us anything at all, it's that sometimes things happen when they do out of sheer random chance.

Which brings us to the part where apologists really back themselves into a corner via a startling bit of circular logic. If everything that begins to exist must have a cause and the universe must have had a beginning because actual infinities are metaphysically impossible, where did God come from? As mentioned earlier, the original formulation of the Cosmological Argument stated that everything that *exists* must have a cause, but modern apologists changed that to everything that *begins to exist* must have a cause. This provided them with a loophole to state that God is exempt from the first premise since he didn't actually *have* a beginning and therefore didn't need a cause to begin to exist.

Well, aside from the fact that this leads to all sort of mental wrangling described above whereby you have to claim that, in order to never have had a beginning, God must simultaneously be an immaterial being consisting of pure "mind" (whatever that means) existing outside of space and time **and** somehow be able to interact with space and time whenever he wants, it also ignores the second premise of the argument that claims that the universe must have had a beginning because an actual infinity is impossible. If that is actually true, then it would also apply to God. Claiming that God, being an infinite and eternal being, is the exception to the rule that actual infinities are impossible is just a case of special pleading and one would be equally justified claiming that the universe (or multiverse) is the exception to the rule and therefore there's no need for God. In other words, if the universe necessarily had a beginning then so did God, and no amount of making up claims out of whole cloth that God must be "timeless" can avoid that fact. And remember -- the "timelessness" of God was not an something originally attributed to him in the scriptures, but was instead something ascribed to him as a way of dealing with the flaws in this argument. God never claimed to exist outside of time, but assuming that he must do so is the only way this argument can possibly work. Except that *"timelessness" doesn't actually mean anything.* If an "actual infinity" is meaningless, the concept of "timelessness" is surely far, far worse. Calling God timeless to patch up a flaw in the KCA is like making up the concept of magical white feathers in my black swan argument described above. Sure, it makes the argument work, but it's ridiculous and self-contradictory on its face and is only required because you want to accept a false premise as true.

But let's go a step further and assume that somehow there is such a thing as an immaterial mind that is both "timeless" and "spaceless" and that such a concept is not just an obvious self-contradiction *[Q: What do you call something that does not exist within space and time? A: Nothing]*. And let's push accommodation to the very limits and assume that such a being could actually somehow interact with the physical universe, at least to the extent of creating it in the first place. What justification is there to imagine that intelligent being just happens to be the God worshiped by your particular religion and not that of your neighbor? One you've "proved" that the universe has a cause and that cause was some sort of intelligent being of some sort, how do you know it's *your* God?

My favorite part of watching people argue for the existence of their particular God using the Kalām Cosmological Argument is when they get to the end and are inevitably asked how they know that this "first cause" God is their particular God. And then you invariably get answers along the line of "Because Christ came to me and spoke to my heart" or "that's where faith comes in" or "the Koran is the most demonstrably true book ever written", etc. In other words, every different religion that believes in a God can use the same argument to prove the existence of their particular version of God, and every different religion is convinced that their version of God is the correct one.

All of which is to say, of course, that an argument that can be used to prove inherently contradictory conclusions is not a particularly useful argument, as illustrated by the following:

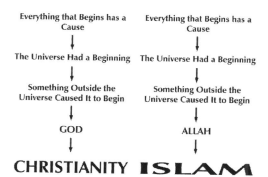

IF THE SAME ARGUMENT CAN BE USED TO PROVE TWO DIFFERENT CONCLUSIONS, THERE'S PROBABLY SOMETHING WRONG WITH THE ARGUMENT

In Conclusion...

So, to sum up:

1. The Cosmological Argument doesn't necessarily prove that the universe must have had any sort of "cause."

2. Even if the universe *did* have a cause, there's no justification to claim that this cause must have been a conscious agent and it makes no sense to describe that cause as somehow "existing outside of space and time" (since the expressions "outside of space" and "outside of time" have no actual meaning) or that it is "pure mind" (since we have no evidence that minds can exist apart from a physical brain) or that something that is outside of space and time could even possibly interact with matter and energy in the first place. After all, when was the last time you were able to affect anything apart from your own body simply by willing it to happen with your mind?

3. Finally, even if the universe *did* have a cause, and even if that cause *could* actually be said to be a timeless, immaterial being of pure mind, there's no justification to associate that being with the God of any particular religion, since it doesn't actually match the description of God from any religion's holy books and has, in fact, been equally associated to many different religions.

A Response to the "Fine-Tuned Universe" Argument

A frequent argument used to prove the existence of God (or some form of God, at least) is the so-called "Fine-Tuned Universe" argument. In a nutshell, the argument is that the universe is so perfectly and improbably "tuned" to support life (human life in particular) that there's no way it could have happened just by chance. Some have phrased the argument more particularly as follows:

The entire universe is governed by 6 mathematical constants:

1. *The ratio of electromagnetic force to gravitational force between two electrons*

2. *The structural constant that determines how various atoms are formed from hydrogen*

3. *The cosmological constant*

4. *The cosmic anti-gravity force*

5. *The value that determines how tightly clusters of galaxies are bound together*

6. *The number of spatial dimensions in the universe*

If the value of any of these constants had been off by even an almost infinitesimal degree, a universe like ours, that's capable of supporting life, would not exist. The odds of each of these constants just happening to all be exactly what is needed to support life, purely by coincidence, is infinitesimally small. Therefore, they must have all been set on purpose by an intelligent being who wanted them to be that way.

There are (at least) four huge problems with the "fine-tuning" argument that I can come up with:

First, the argument assumes that the values of the various constants supposedly required for the universe to be capable of supporting life could, in fact, have possibly been different than what they actually are. It's not "fine-tuning" if there were no other options available.

Second, there's a huge difference between "capable of sustaining life" and "capable of sustaining life as we know it." Even if the various constants could have had some other values, who is to say that some other form of life wouldn't have arisen instead? In other words, it's more accurate to say that life evolved to fit the way the universe is rather than saying the universe was designed to support the life that would eventually evolve within it.

Third, for a universe that is supposedly "finely tuned" to support life, it seems awfully strange that the vast majority of said universe is not, in fact, capable of sustaining life. Even here on Earth, there are plenty of regions totally inhospitable to life. And what about all the other planets in the solar system? And the vast emptiness of interstellar space? What about planets near supernovas and black holes?

Finally, what makes life so special? Why not say the universe has been finely tuned to support the existence of diamonds? Or black holes? Or the rings around Saturn? All of these things (let alone the vast multitude of non-human life on this planet such as insects) are also only possible because the universe is exactly the way it is.

I like to compare the fine-tuning argument to the odds of my own existence given the vagaries of my ancestry. In order for me to be here in exactly the way I am, every one of my ancestors over the entire course of human history must have met and mated with the exact right person. If my great-great-grandmother on my father's side had married the boy her parents had forbidden her to marry instead of the man they approved of, I might have a different shaped nose, no genetic disposition to diabetes, bigger feet, etc. Or I might not have been born at all. In fact, given the size of the human population throughout time and the size of the mating pool, the odds of every single one of my ancestors mating with the exact person they did is so ridiculously low that it can't have happened by chance.

No, it's crystal clear that some external force must have been guiding each and every ancestor from the dawn of time until my mother met my father, ensuring that they met and mated exactly on schedule (did I mention the two miscarriages my mother had before having me?) In fact, given the fact that many of my ancestors traveled across the globe before meeting each other due to various political upheavals, I think it's fair to say that the majority of human history was manipulated by this external force in order to ensure that I would be born exactly the way I was, small feet, diabetes and all.

Except, of course, that had anything been different in the past then the outcome would have been different and I wouldn't be here discussing it. If you tried to estimate in advance (say, 10,000 years ago) the odds of me coming out exactly the way I did, the odds would be ridiculously, impossibly small. But if you try to estimate the odds now of me turning out the way I did based on my past ancestry, the odds are exactly 1:1.

Another analogy I have heard compares the improbability of the universe turning out just the way it did to the improbability of someone dealing out a shuffled deck of cards and just happening to lay down a complete suit (e.g., all clubs, all hearts, etc.). From a purely mathematical standpoint, the odds of doing this from a shuffled deck of cards are 635,013,559,600 to one. Which is, of course, incredibly improbable and you would be right to suspect that the dealer had somehow rigged the deck in his favor.

Except… let's say I deal out thirteen cards from a shuffled deck and get a totally random mixture of hearts, clubs, diamonds and spades. What are the odds that I laid down the exact combination of cards that I did? Still 635,013,559,600 to one. How can this happen? Well, it's all because 635 billion to 1 against was the chance of getting it right before the cards were dealt. In fact, now they've been dealt, the probability is actually 1. Talking about how improbable something was that has actually happened already is not helpful.

Similarly, one can look at a lottery where the odds of any one person winning may be 250,000,000 to 1, but the probability of somebody winning the lottery is pretty close to 1:1 before the drawing and exactly 1 after somebody actually does win it.

In terms of the universe, nobody was around before it began to estimate the probability that things would be as they are today. Had there been someone, then they'd have calculated a very, very slim probability indeed. But here's a universe and here we are in it. The probability of this having occurred is exactly 1:1. Again, there are two possibilities. Either the universe was made just to suit life, or else life evolved to fit the way the universe is.

One other point to consider… Let's assume that the "fine-tuned universe" argument *is* actually correct and that the odds of the universe turning out the way it did by chance are mind-bogglingly, infinitesimally small (further assuming that it did, in fact, happen by chance and not because of some immutable laws of nature). How can you say that the odds are any better of it being created by some timeless, immaterial being whose very nature would contradict all we know about existence? How would you even go about calculating those odds? Regardless of how unlikely a naturally caused universe is, you have to first show that a supernatural cause is even **possible** before you can argue that it is plausible (let alone more probable than a naturally caused universe).

A Response to the Ontological Argument for the Existence of God

I originally wasn't going to bother even mentioning this particular argument since (a) as originally formulated the argument seems so laughably inadequate that it really doesn't bear much discussion in the first place and (b) modern formulations of the argument add so much jargon and technical word-play that it can be very difficult to even understand what the argument actually is by the time you finish reading it. I will admit, however, that the original ontological argument was seen as significant enough in the past that numerous famous philosophers such as Kant, Hume and even Saint Thomas Aquinas took the time to object to it, so perhaps it's not as laughably inadequate as it appears to me.

As originally formulated by theologian and philosopher Anselm of Canterbury (1033–1109), the ontological argument is as follows:

1. It is a conceptual truth (or, so to speak, true by definition) that God is a being than which none greater can be imagined (that is, the greatest possible being that can be imagined).

2. God exists as an idea in the mind.

3. A being that exists as an idea in the mind and in reality is, other things being equal, greater than a being that exists only as an idea in the mind.

4. Thus, if God exists only as an idea in the mind, then we can imagine something that is greater than God (that is, a greatest possible being that does exist).

5. But we cannot imagine something that is greater than God (for it is a contradiction to suppose that we can imagine a being greater than the greatest possible being that can be imagined.)

6. Therefore, God exists.

He later restated this same argument slightly differently:

1. By definition, God is a being than which none greater can be imagined.

2. A being that necessarily exists in reality is greater than a being that does not necessarily exist.

3. Thus, by definition, if God exists as an idea in the mind but does not necessarily exist in reality, then we can imagine something that is greater than God.

4. But we cannot imagine something that is greater than God.

5. Thus, if God exists in the mind as an idea, then God necessarily exists in reality.

6. God exists in the mind as an idea.

7. Therefore, God necessarily exists in reality.

As we all know (or should know by now) an argument is only as good as its premises, and a perfectly *valid* argument can be completely *unsound* if the premises are not actually true.

The first premise of the ontological argument is that, **by definition**, God is the greatest possible being that can be imagined. This sinks the entire argument right from the start, since it is *defining* God as "the greatest possible thing that can be imagined" without actually providing any empirical evidence that this is the case. It is also setting up a wholly circular argument by arbitrarily defining God as a being that embodies the very characteristic that will later be used to prove His existence. You might as well define "unicorns" as "the beings responsible for the color blue" and then claim that the existence of the color blue is therefore proof that unicorns exist. This is simply defining God into existence, since we don't actually know what God is like even if He were to exist and it basically amounts to an argument that states, "God, by definition, exists; therefore, He exists."

The second premise that a being that exists (or "necessarily exists," if you prefer) is more perfect than one that doesn't exist is yet another assertion without any evidence to support it. How does one even define "perfect" in the first place? If I want to go all Platonic, should I start claiming that the "perfect" concept of a chair, to which all actual chairs are merely compared to in our mind, must somehow actually exist somewhere or else it can't actually be "perfect"? Of course not. "Perfection" is, in many cases, an ideal that does not actually exist and there is no requirement to think that something *must* exist in order to be considered perfect. Just *asserting* that something that exists is "more perfect" than something that is only a concept doesn't make it so.

Aside from the fact that this entire argument is nothing more than an attempt to define God into existence, however, this argument suffers from the same problem as many of the other arguments I mentioned above. To wit, at most all these arguments can *possibly* prove is that *some sort* of supreme being exists and not the actual "God" that is actually worshiped by those who would use these arguments to prove their God's existence. The God supposedly proved by these arguments is **not** the God that answers prayers, performs miracles, provides revelation, rewards the faithful, punishes sinners, gives us a set of objective morals, tells us the way to live our lives, etc. It is a nebulous description of God that could apply equally to the God worshiped by *any* religion, and therefore cannot be used to prove the existence of the God worshiped by any *specific* religion. It's the ultimate bait and switch.

A Response to Aquinas's "Five Ways"

This is another argument (or set of related arguments) that I originally hadn't planned to bother with, simply because I honestly didn't think anybody took them seriously anymore due to how old they are how frequently they have been refuted since first proposed by Catholic philosopher/apologist Thomas Aquinas back in the 1200s. However, due to the number of times I have specifically be asked to address this, I figured I might as well at least give a brief overview of why these arguments are generally no longer offered as proof of anything.

The first three of Aquinas's five "ways" borrow heavily from Aristotle (an ancient Greek philosopher who was definitely *not* a Christian) and are all basically restatements of the so-called "cosmological argument" that argues that *something* must have initially set the universe into motion, been the "first cause," etc. The primary flaws in these arguments are the unfounded assertions that make up the premises. For example, the assertion that our observations regarding how things operate *within* the universe must also apply to the universe as a whole. Or the assertion that an infinite regression is actually impossible.

More importantly, each of these three arguments close by stating that this *something* that has supposedly been proved to exist is "understood by everybody to be God," which is simply not the case. Even if it were possible to logically prove that *something* was responsible for the beginning of the universe and causing everything to exist, there is nothing to show that this *something* must necessarily be any sort of intelligent being, let alone that it is the God actually worshiped by any particular religion.

The fourth "way" argues that the only way we are able to make value judgments about anything in life being "better" or "worse" the other things is by comparing things to some standard of perfection and determining whether the things are "more" or "less" good than that standard. This is borrowed from Plato (another Greek philosopher who was not a Christian) and his concept of "ideals". However, it really is just word play and an attempt to define God into existence. You don't need a "perfect" standard to compare two things and judge that one is better than the other for a specific purpose. A chair without a broken leg is better than a chair with a broken leg because one lets you sit and the other dumps you on the ground. No appeal to some perfect standard of goodness required. Plus, once again, Aquinas says that this perfect standard against which all ideas of "good" are judged is "understood by everybody to be God," which once again is simply not the case.

The fifth and final "way" can be summarized as follows:

> *We see various non-intelligent objects in the world behaving in regular ways. This cannot be due to chance since then they would not behave with predictable results. So their behavior must be set. But it cannot be set by themselves since they are non-intelligent and have no notion of how to set behavior. Therefore, their behavior must be set by something else, and by implication something that must be intelligent. This everyone understands to be God.*

>   -- Five Ways (Aquinas) - Wikipedia

This whole argument is based on ignorance of any method by which non-intelligent objects can behave in regular ways without divine intervention and/or design. Our discovery of natural laws such as gravity and natural selection, however, completely debunk this initial premise. We now know that natural laws can work on random events in a non-random way. Oh — and once again, Aquinas just asserts that whatever it is that supposedly causes non-intelligent objects to behave in regular ways is understood by everybody to be God.

The bottom line is that each of Aquinas's Five Ways are unsound arguments that rely on unsupported premises to reach a conclusion that doesn't actually match the God he is arguing for due to being overly broad.

It is also important to note that Aquinas's purpose in providing these arguments was not necessarily intended to prove to nonbelievers that God exists, but instead to "help Dominicans not enrolled in the university prepare for their priestly duties of preaching and hearing confessions by systematizing Catholic truth utilizing mainly Aristotelean tools" (Christopher M. Brown, "'Summa Theologiae' by Thomas Aquinas"). Therefore, anybody who uses these arguments today in an attempt to prove the existence of God does so at their own peril (including the risk of being laughed at).

On a more humorous note, the following is an analogy I came up with to show just how flawed Aquinas's reasoning is, especially when he keeps asserting, "This everyone understands to be God":

1. There are pumpkins in the world.

2. For every pumpkin that we observe, there exists the possibility that there is another pumpkin bigger than it.

3. This cannot be true of every pumpkin, however, since that would lead to an infinite regression of pumpkins.

4. Therefore, there must be one pumpkin that is bigger than any other pumpkin could ever possibly be.

5. **Everybody understands this to be the Great Pumpkin.**

[Apologies to Charles Schulz]

A Response to the "Trilemma" Argument (a.k.a the "Liar, Lunatic or Lord" Proof for the Existence of God)

This is yet another argument that I honestly didn't think needed to be addressed due to how obviously flimsy it is, but once again it is one that still manages to pop up on a distressingly regular basis.

Most of the various Christian apologetic arguments for the existence of God used today are rather ancient, dating back in many cases all the way to the time of the ancient Greek philosophers who actually predated Christ entirely and were arguing for the existence of completely different gods than the one described in the Christian Bible. One more modern argument, however, is commonly referred to as the "Trilemma" argument and was popularized by British author C.S. Lewis in his book "Mere Christianity" written in the 1950s.

Lewis's formulation of the argument is as follows:

> *I am trying here to prevent anyone saying the really foolish thing that people often say about Him: I'm ready to accept Jesus as a great moral teacher, but I don't accept his claim to be God. That is the one thing we must not say. A man who was merely a man and said the sort of things Jesus said would not be a great moral teacher. He would either be a lunatic — on the level with the man who says he is a poached egg — or else he would be the Devil of Hell. You must make your choice. Either this man was, and is, the Son of God, or else a madman or something worse. You can shut him up for a fool, you can spit at him and kill him as a demon or you can fall at his feet and call him Lord and God, but let us not come with any patronizing nonsense about his being a great human teacher. He has not left that open to us. He did not intend to. ... Now it seems to me obvious that He was neither a lunatic nor a fiend: and consequently, however*

strange or terrifying or unlikely it may seem, I have to accept the view that He was and is God.

Scots preacher John Duncan put it this way about a century earlier:

Christ either deceived mankind by conscious fraud, or He was Himself deluded and self-deceived, or He was Divine. There is no getting out of this trilemma. It is inexorable.

And modern apologists usually just refer to this idea as the "Liar, Lord or Lunatic" argument for the divinity of Jesus.

Now, it may be easy to dismiss this entire argument by simply saying that maybe Christ was, indeed, either a liar or a lunatic. But implicit in the argument is the idea that those two choices can be rejected for some reason, leaving only the third choice as a viable option. Lewis himself stated that, "It seems to me obvious that He was neither a lunatic nor a fiend," which really doesn't prove anything since what is "obvious" to him may not be obvious to others or actually true. But other modern Christian apologists have expounded on this idea and claimed that the historical record itself (a.k.a. The Bible) shows that Christ's actions were described as actually being witnessed by other people, thereby ruling out the possibility that he was merely a liar. In addition, the fact that so many people chose to follow his teachings and the church build upon his name has lasted millennia rules out the possibility that he was merely a lunatic spouting nonsense.

Personally, I don't think there is actually any good reason to say that Christ, if he even lived at all, was *not* a liar or a lunatic. People lie about things all the time and people also believe in all sorts of crazy things. But let's just accept, for the sake of argument, the thought that we can somehow rule out those two options. Does that really leave us with the only possible option being that Christ really was a divine being, the Son of God?

No, don't be ridiculous.

Even if you assume that it is actually a fact that "the man Jesus existed" (something for which we do not actually know for sure) and that he was neither a liar nor a lunatic, consider the following:

We know from the historical record that the man Vlad Dracula existed. Many years after his death, an author by the name of Bram Stoker wrote a book based on this historic figure in which the main character claimed to be an undead vampire who could turn into various animals and even into mist.

Now, given that the man Dracula actually existed, would you accept that he must have either been a liar, a madman or actually an undead vampire who could change into animals and mist? And, further, that since his actions were described as being witnessed by other people in that book (ruling out the possibility that he was merely a liar or a madman), he must therefore have really been an undead vampire who could change into animals and mist?

Or do you think that maybe, just *maybe*, the book "Dracula" was just a fictional account of a real historical figure doing fictional things with fictional witnesses attesting to those things?

[Oh — and just for the record, Abraham Lincoln never actually fought any vampires, despite the fact that he was a real historical person and despite the fact that somebody wrote a book claiming that he fought vampires. Just saying.]

The bottom line is that, even if Christ actually existed as a historical person, we have no way of knowing whether he actually said or did *any* of the things attributed to him by anonymous authors who wrote stories about his life many decades after he supposedly lived and died. We have no actual writings attributed to Christ himself, and many Biblical scholars believe that the four "Gospels" describing what he said and did were written *after* Paul started going around telling people about his vision of a risen Christ as a way of providing some backstory for the Church Paul was working to start. And so, of course, these authors scoured the Jewish Tanakh (the so-called "Old Testament") and tried to cram as much relevant details into their stories as possible to make it look as though Christ was fulfilling ancient prophecies and performing miraculous acts.

In other words, the whole "trilemma" argument is just a way of cheating by excluding any other possibilities. If you want to keep the alliteration, you could say that it really needs to be a "quadlemma" with the choices being "Liar, Lunatic, Lord or **Legend**."

As an aside, many people who have studied this issue over the years have questioned why a seemingly well-educated and otherwise rational man such as C.S. Lewis would commit such an astoundingly obvious logical fallacy as the False Dilemma (in which a statement falsely claims an "either/or" situation, when in fact there is at least one additional logically valid option). To explain this, I have come up with very own "trilemma" of choices:

*C.S. Lewis was either **Deluded, Duplicitous** or **Desperate**.*

And by "desperate" I am referring to the extreme sort of wishful thinking that many believers engage in when they just really, really *want* their beliefs to be true so they don't have to deal with the realities of life and death.

I don't think that Lewis was being purposely duplicitous and would hesitate to call him "deluded" (although a bit of self-delusion is probably involved here), so that only leaves "desperate" as the explanation. Because, of course, there can't possibly be any other possible explanation other than the three choices I laid out, right?

A Response to the "Minimal Facts" Argument

The so-called "Minimal Facts" argument is occasionally offered by Christian apologists in an attempt to show that it is logical to believe the God of the Bible exists (if not as outright proof that He does). It has two main premises:

1. There are certain historical facts regarding Jesus and the early days of Christianity that are universally accepted by all critical scholars.
2. These facts can best be explained by the existence of a God as described in the Christian Bible.

With regard to premise #1, the facts are said to be "confirmed by several strong and independent arguments, plus the vast majority of even critical scholars must recognize the occurrence's historical nature." Furthermore, the so-called "critical scholars" can be "liberal, skeptical, agnostic, or even atheist, *as long as they are specialists in a relevant field of study*, such as New Testament."

The actual list of facts is generally presented as follows:

1. that Jesus *died by crucifixion*
2. that very soon afterwards, his followers had *real experiences* that they thought were actual appearances of the risen Jesus
3. that their lives were *transformed* as a result, even to the point of being willing to die specifically for their faith in the resurrection message
4. that these things were *taught very early*, soon after the crucifixion
5. that *James*, Jesus' unbelieving brother, became a Christian due to his own experience that he thought was the resurrected Christ
6. that the Christian persecutor *Paul* (formerly Saul of Tarsus) also became a believer after a similar experience.

Without attempting to rebut each and every one of these supposed "facts" in detail, allow me to just point out two major flaws with this argument as a whole:

1. The supposed facts are *not*, in fact, universally accepted (even by so-called "critical scholars"). Although there may be some slight evidence that somebody named Jesus actually lived around 2000 years ago and may have had a following, there is zero accepted historical evidence for the first three "facts" at all. There is simply no way to tell whether anybody who lived 2000 years ago had a "real" experience, whether they lied about an experience they had, or whether they are wholly fictional people in the first place. The rest of the "facts" are equally unsupported.
2. Even if all the "facts" were actually true, there is no justification for claiming that "God" is the best explanation. This is like seeing a strange light in the sky that you can't explain and claiming that the "best" explanation is that the light is actually a spacecraft piloted by aliens from the Andromeda galaxy. Sure, that is one possible explanation, but it requires so many assumptions that are counter to experience that it can hardly be said to be the "best" explanation.

But What About All the Miracles?

Frequently, atheists get challenged by theists to justify their lack of belief in the face of all the "obvious" or "well-documented" or "clearly factual" accounts of miracles throughout history. Sometimes this challenge comes in response to an atheist claim that there is no evidence to support a belief in God, and sometimes it just comes out of the blue as an attack on atheists by some theist who just can't understand how somebody could not share what they "know" to be true. Often, but not always, the challenge is accompanied by a laundry list of alleged "miracles" ranging from the blandly general ("God created the universe!" "God created life!") to the weirdly specific ("I opened up a fortune cookie and found the message 'God will help you overcome any hardship' while on a planned trip to receive medical treatment") and everything in-between.

Playing whack-a-mole with individual miraculous claims is not a particularly good way to spend one's time, since the believer will likely just reject any counter-evidence or explanation you may offer to that particular claim and/or say, "Well, OK, but what about *this* miracle?" So, instead, let me just give some general thoughts on miraculous claims in general here.

First of all, atheists (and, for that matter, members of other religions who don't accept the truth of the particular religion making the particular claim) can explain miraculous claims as being any of the following:

- An **anecdotal story** with no supporting evidence that therefore has no probative value whatsoever. This includes ancient lore passed down through generations and/or written down in a holy book, as well as "faith promoting stories" circulated among members of a community of the faithful.

- A **misinterpretation** or **misattribution** of actual events. Coincidences are powerful things, and it's all too easy to fall into the trap of Confirmation bias, whereby we tend to focus on the coincidences that support our beliefs and ignore or discount all the times that things happened that didn't support our beliefs. There's also the common *Post hoc ergo propter* hoc fallacy, whereby we tend to think that just because one event came after a previous event (say, that somebody got better after praying for a miracle), the first event must have been the *cause* of the second event. Finally, when we have a positive event in our lives, there is a tendency to attribute that event to our chosen cause regardless of what the "real" cause was ("After five months of chemotherapy and radiation treatment, my cancer finally went into remission thanks to God's blessing").

- A flat-out **lie** or **deception**. Whether you want to call it a "faith-promoting story", Lying for Jesus™ or just an effort to separate the gullible from their hard-earned cash, the fact remains that people make stuff up all the time. It doesn't matter if it was your beloved aunt who told you the story or whether it was the leader of your congregation. It doesn't matter if you read it on a website somewhere, saw it in a YouTube video or even read about it in a newspaper. People can and do lie.

Second of all, even if a particular miraculous claim cannot be shown to either be an unsupported anecdotal story, a misinterpretation or misattribution of actual events, or a flat-out lie or deception, there's still a question as to what such "miraculous" events could properly prove in the first place. To say that, for example, a person was healed of a supposedly incurable disease in a way that science cannot explain — even if true — just proves that science cannot (yet) explain how the person was cured, not that "God did it."

Similarly, if science cannot explain how the universe first began or how life on earth formed or how consciousness is possible or whatever, that doesn't provide a shred of evidence that the particular God that somebody happens to believe in (out of all the many different gods that have been worshiped throughout history, mind you) must therefore be the cause. It just means that, yes, science cannot (yet) explain it.

And What About All the Answered Prayers?

In addition to being challenged to explain how miracles are possible if there is no God, atheists are often asked to explain how prayers get answered if God doesn't exist.

Well, here's a challenge for anybody who thinks that the particular deity they were most likely indoctrinated from an early age to believe in has actually ever answered their prayers:

Take a gallon milk jug, fill it up with sand, paint it bright red, and stick it on your kitchen counter. And then, every single day, ask that jug for something different that you want. Maybe one day ask for a sick family member to get better, maybe ask to be able to find a better job, maybe ask for your annoying neighbor to stop letting his dog poop on your lawn every day, whatever. It doesn't matter. Just make sure to ask for something every day.

Now, here are the rules:

1. You must believe that the jug will *always* answer your request, one way or another.

2. If something happens that you asked the jug for (even if it didn't happen immediately or exactly in the way you expected), you must accept that the jug heard your request and used its magic to answer it in the affirmative.

3. If something *doesn't* happen that you asked the jug for, you must accept that the jug heard your request and either hasn't *yet* used its magic to grant it (in which case you need

to be more patient) or else has decided not to grant it at all for reasons of its own. If the latter, you must accept that your request was not ignored — the answer was simply "no."

Now, given these rules, how long do you think before you can confidently state that the jug did, in fact, answer one of your requests (either in the affirmative or the negative)?

OK, now stop asking requests of the magic milk jug and try the same exact experiment with a magical being that you imagine exists somewhere in the sky. Do you imagine the results will be any different, given the same exact set of rules?

Does Scientifically Accurate Information in a Holy Book Prove the Existence of God?

Most theists are perfectly happy to acknowledge that their religion's holy book is primarily meant to be taken metaphorically and isn't supposed to be any sort of science book. These tend to be the same theists who acknowledge that the truth of God's existence must be taken on faith (an inherently irrational experience) and that there isn't any objective evidence of God's existence as a result.

Some theists, however, apparently really hate the thought of being "looked down upon" by rational atheists and therefore constantly look for anything that can be offered as evidence (if not actual proof) of their God's existence. And one form of this behavior is the assertion that their particular religion's holy book is just chock-full of amazingly accurate scientific information that couldn't possibly have been known at the time the book was written. And the only explanation, of course, is that the information was provided directly by God and this proves that God exists.

Now, there are three main problems with these sorts of assertions. First of all, these assertions are made by Christians to prove that the Bible is true (and therefore Christianity is true and therefore the God of the Christian Bible is real), but also by Muslims to prove that the Qur'an is true (and therefore Islam is true and therefore the Allah is real) and even by some Hindus to prove the Vedas are true (and therefore Hinduism is true and one or more of the many deities worshiped by Hindus are real). That doesn't prove that one of those books *isn't* a miraculous work of one deity or another, but any "proof" that can be used to prove three contradictory claims probably isn't worth much.

[As an aside, these claims about a particular religion's holy book being full of impossibly accurate scientific information always seem to be addressed to atheists and not members of other religions who make similar claims about their holy books. I'd love to lock a fundamentalist Christian and fundamentalist Muslim in a room together and let them toss the same exact arguments at each other to prove that their *holy book (but not the other's holy book, of course) must be true. And then maybe film it and post it on YouTube...]*

Second of all, it's awfully suspicious that nobody ever seems to notice these scientifically accurate passages (or, more properly, realize what they supposedly "really" mean) until *after* modern science has made a particular discovery. It's always a case of science making a discovery and then people going back and looking for passages that can possibly be interpreted to agree with that discovery. Kind of. Sort of. If you squint *just* right.

Third of all, the passages quoted usually don't even say what the theists claim that they say unless you add all sorts of unwarranted assumptions, ignore the plain meaning of the language, ignore all the parts that are blatantly wrong and, once again, squint *really* hard.

Some Christians, for example, love to claim that the beginning of Genesis ("And God said let there be light") is somehow a scientifically accurate description of what we now generally refer to as the "big bang" (the time when the early universe began to rapidly expand from an initial hot and dense state). Except cosmologists now say that the first visible light didn't appear until 300,000 years *after* that initial expansion. And what about the other parts of the same chapter that talk about scientifically *inaccurate* things like plants appearing before the sun was created?

Similarly, some Muslims claim that nonsense such as the following is a 100% accurate and true description of human embryological development:

> *Man We did create from a quintessence of clay. Then we placed him as a drop of sperm in a place of rest, firmly fixed. Then We made the sperm into a clot of congealed blood. Then out of that clot We made a fetus lump. Then We made out of that lump bones, and clothed the bones with flesh. Then We developed out of it another creature. So blessed be Allah, the Best to create! (23:12-14).*

That doesn't appear to be even *remotely* similar to how actual embryology is now known to work, however. What about the role the ovum plays in all of this? What spot of congealed blood? And why does it say the bones are created first and then covered with flesh when we now know that the fetus is covered with flesh before bones develop? And no, it really doesn't matter that one (and only one) non-Muslim embryologist once gave a speech claiming that it was an accurate description after he was paid a lot of money by the Saudi government to do so. When one (and only one) expert out of many thousands voices an opinion that supports your belief, it takes an extreme form of confirmation bias to think that actually means anything.

Now, with regards to Christians thinking the Bible contains impossibly accurate scientific information in particular, it's interesting to note that some of the earliest and most important Church Fathers had some pretty harsh words to say about those who would take the words of the Bible as scientifically accurate descriptions of the world instead of acknowledging them for the metaphorical descriptions that they were intended to be. For example:

> *Usually, even a non-Christian knows something about the earth, the heavens, and the other elements of this world, about the motion and orbit of the stars and even their size and relative positions, about the predictable eclipses of the sun and moon, the cycles of the years and the seasons, about the kinds of animals, shrubs, stones, and so forth, and this knowledge he hold to as being certain from reason and experience. Now, it is a disgraceful and dangerous thing for an infidel to hear a Christian, presumably giving the meaning of Holy Scripture, talking nonsense on these topics; and we should take all means to prevent such an embarrassing situation, in which people show up vast ignorance in a Christian and laugh it to scorn. The shame is not so much that an ignorant individual is derided, but that people outside the household of faith think our sacred writers held such opinions, and, to the great loss of those for whose salvation we toil, the writers of our Scripture are criticized and rejected as unlearned men. If they find a Christian mistaken in a field which they themselves know well and hear him maintaining his foolish opinions about our books, how are they going to believe those books in matters concerning the resurrection of the dead, the hope of eternal life, and the kingdom of heaven, when they think their pages are full of falsehoods and on facts which they themselves have learnt from experience and the light of reason? **Reckless and incompetent expounders of Holy Scripture bring untold trouble and sorrow on their wiser brethren when they***

are caught in one of their mischievous false opinions and are taken to task by those who are not bound by the authority of our sacred books. For then, to defend their utterly foolish and obviously untrue statements, they will try to call upon Holy Scripture for proof and even recite from memory many passages which they think support their position, although they understand neither what they say nor the things about which they make assertion.

— St Augustine of Hippo (A.D 354 - 430): The literal meaning of Genesis (De Genesi ad litteram libro duodecim)

And an even *earlier* Church father had this to say:

For who that has understanding will suppose that the first, and second, and third day, and the evening and the morning, existed without a sun, and moon, and stars? And that the first day was, as it were, also without a sky? And who is so foolish as to suppose that God, after the manner of a husbandman, planted a paradise in Eden, towards the east, and placed in it a tree of life, visible and palpable, so that one tasting of the fruit by the bodily teeth obtained life? And again, that one was a partaker of good and evil by masticating what was taken from the tree? And if God is said to walk in the paradise in the evening, and Adam to hide himself under a tree, I do not suppose that anyone doubts that these things figuratively indicate certain mysteries, the history having taken place in appearance, and not literally.

— Origen (c. 184 – c. 253), *On the First Principles*

Just something to keep in mind and perhaps remind Christians of the next time they try this particular argument.

Does the Beauty and Majesty of the Natural World Prove that God Exists?

A question that gets frequently asked of atheists is, "How can we possibly look at all the wonders of the natural world and **not** believe in God?" Now, sure, this is partially just a restatement of the classic "Argument from Design" (see _A Response to the Argument from Design_ on p.81), and it also involves a fair amount of arguing from ignorance or personal incredulity ("I can't personally imagine how such a thing is possible without God, therefore it must not be possible"). But I think it actually goes a little deeper than that.

After all, once upon a time, we really _did_ have no idea what caused sunsets, how mountains formed, how rock structures came to look like they were carved into interesting shapes, etc., so it only made sense to think that such things were specifically created for our benefit. But now we obviously are able to explain how all these things are caused by purely natural forces and principles, so this question can't just be due to sheer ignorance of how the natural world works. There must be more to it than that.

But hey — maybe all this means is that God created all the natural laws in the first place and therefore is ultimately responsible for it turning out the way it has. Sure, God didn't _personally_ sculpt the amazing rock formations seen in Utah's Zion National Park or the Grand Canyon, but can't we still give Him the credit for creating the rocks and wind and water and setting up a natural system whereby rocks can be eroded by wind and water? And sure, maybe God doesn't _personally_ paint every single beautiful sunset by hand, but we can still praise Him for creating the water cycles that causes clouds to form and making it so that sunlight refracts when it strikes water droplets, etc., right? And, OK, so maybe God didn't _personally_ cause those majestic mountains to rise out of the crust and get covered with snow, but we can still worship Him for coming up with the idea of plate tectonics and snow in the first place, right? After all, God created the entire universe from scratch, and therefore every beautiful and awesome and great thing we see in that universe must therefore be the result of God's will, right?

So, maybe the argument is not simply about how could all these things exist without God but instead why would they all be so majestic and beautiful and awe-inspiring without God. Surely God must have set things up so that the end results would be so amazing, right?

OK, let's play that game. The natural world is full of amazing, beautiful, wonderful and awe-inspiring things that prove that God exists and loves us enough to share all this beauty with us. Gotcha. Now let's take a look at all the things in the natural world that *aren't* so great, shall we? Let's look at the volcanic eruptions instead of just looking at the majestic mountains. Let's look at the vast dust storms instead of just looking at the pretty sunsets. Let's look at the floods and earthquakes and droughts and lightning strikes and tornadoes and hurricanes and tsunamis instead of just looking at the amazing rock formations. And then go look at the children dying of genetic diseases and the ugliness of things like Ebola and smallpox and parasitic infections and flesh-eating bacteria. Care to look at some picture of people with half of their face eaten off? Seriously — go ahead and do a Google image search for flesh-eating bacteria. It's OK, I'll wait for you to finish vomiting at the sight and come back here.

.

.

.

Still with me? Wonderful. Now, after looking at all that ugliness in the world, you go ahead and tell me that it's all a testament to just how depraved and sadistic and cruel God is, since He created the universe from scratch and therefore every horrible and ugly and terrible thing we see in that universe must also be the result of God's will.

- No, you can't claim that the ugliness is just random stuff not under God's direct control or all the work of Satan.

- No, you can't claim that all the bad stuff is the result of man's exercise of free will, since I didn't even mention anything related to man's inhumanity to man.
- No, you can't claim that Adam and Eve sinned and somehow caused the entire universe to enter a "fallen" state since (a) that would mean that a supposedly loving God decided to punish the entire universe for the sins of two people and (b) it would also negate all the previously "great" things that you previously gave God credit for. I mean, seriously — either the world is full of ugliness because it is in a fallen state or else it is full of beauty and greatness because of God. You can't have it both ways.

So, please. Go ahead. You admit that all the ugliness in the world is evidence that God is a sadistic bastard (or, perhaps doesn't exist at all), and I'll admit that the beauty in the natural world is evidence that He does exist and loves us so much that He wants to share His glory with us. You don't get to just look at the good and ignore the bad and claim that it somehow proves something.

[Having said all that, let me just make it clear that I *do* think there are many beautiful, majestic and awe-inspiring sights in the natural world, both here on earth and out in the rest of the known universe. And no, I don't think the entire universe is a dark and depressing place just because there are also many ugly, hideous and scary things as well. I take the good with the bad and understand that this is what happens when you have a universe that operates on impersonal natural principles and that wasn't designed specifically for our benefit.]

Does All of Creation Prove the Existence of a Creator?

For those theists who aren't content with just acknowledging that faith is an inherently irrational process that involves believing in something despite a lack of evidence (and sometimes even despite evidence to the contrary), one frequent bit of "evidence" that gets offered to support their belief in whatever deity they were most likely indoctrinated from a young age to believe in is that all of creation somehow necessarily proves the existence of a creator. After all, you can't have a creation without a creator, right? And what else could we possibly call the creator of the entire universe except "God" (and, more particularly, whichever "God" the person making this argument was most likely indoctrinated from a young age to believe in, of course).

Although related to the classic Argument from Design (see _A Response to the Argument from Design_ on p.81), that argument relies on the apparent _appearance_ of design of things within the universe due to their complexity, whereas this argument is really just a combination of not so clever wordplay combined with a perhaps sincere inability to comprehend how the universe could possibly exist without "God" being responsible.

So, let's break it down a bit, shall we?

First of all, there's the whole bit about all of "creation" necessarily being "created." Yes, the phrase "all of creation" was originally used to specifically imply that everything in the universe was created specifically by God, but in modern English it just means "everything in existence" in the same way that "creature" now just means "a living being" despite the word originally referring to any animal that was "created" (presumably by God).

Second of all, the word "created" is a very loaded term, since it implies the existence of a "creator" and most people think that a "creator" must be some sort of intelligent being. However, this isn't actually the case. When a meteorite strikes the earth and "creates" a crater, it would be appropriate to call the meteorite the "creator" of that crater despite the fact that nobody thinks that meteorites are intelligent beings.

Similarly, when the process of water seeping through limestone over many years "creates" a complex network of stalactites and stalagmites in a cave, it would be appropriate to call that process the "creator" of those stalactites and stalagmites despite the fact that nobody thinks that natural processes are intelligent beings.

Similarly, when a snowflake suddenly appears out of seemingly thin air, we understand that the snowflake formed according to whatever natural laws govern the formation of snowflakes and that the seemingly "thin air" actually contains all the components necessary for that snowflake to form. We don't just say that the snowflake must have been created by magical snowflake fairies who can do impossible things even if we don't understand exactly how they formed:

Third of all, even if you so insist on using use the word "creator" to refer to whatever is responsible for the formation of stars and galaxies or even the universe as a whole, the fact that there is a "creator" says precisely nothing about who or what that creator actually is. As mentioned above, you can label all sorts of things a "creator," including inanimate objects and natural processes, and nothing requires that a "creator" must be an intelligent being of some sort. And it especially doesn't mean it must be whatever specific "God" you were most likely personally indoctrinated from an early age to believe in.

Finally, it's important to remember that the opposite of "Science *can* currently explain something" is "Science *cannot* currently explain something" and not "Therefore, God did it." Lack of a better explanation for something is not any sort of evidence for your preferred explanation, unless you have some independent evidence that your preferred explanation is true. Provide some clear evidence that your particular "God" actually *does* (or even possibly *could*) exist, and then we can have a nice discussion as to whether that God is a good, better or best explanation for anything. Until then, however, offering "God did it" as an explanation is about as "scientific" as claiming that the universe must have been created by a race of hyper-intelligent, pan-dimensional beings who wanted to run a simulation to determine the actual question to the ultimate answer of life, the universe and everything and who, quite incidentally, happen to resemble white mice.[9]

Sorry, Deists — Your God Doesn't Exist Either

In most of my discussions about God and whether or not there is any good reason to believe God exists I have focused on the various concepts of God that people actually worship, since those concepts of God are described as having specific characteristics and as having done and promised to do specific things. As such, those concepts of God make testable claims that we should be able to verify and for which there should be an abundance of reliable and objective evidence, so the complete lack of reliable and objective evidence and the fact that the various claims can and have been proven to be false is, in itself, compelling evidence that those concepts of God do not, in fact, exist.

With such a focus on evidence and counter-evidence, however, I have often more or less given a pass to the concept of the so-called "Deist" God. The Deist God is described as the Creator of the Universe (as with most theistic concepts of God), but with the qualification that this Creator simply set the universe in motion and then let it run on its own ever since with absolutely no further interference whatsoever. This means that the Deist God has never revealed itself to humanity in any way, does not perform miracles, does not provide moral guidance, does not promise salvation, etc. And the reason I have more or less given a pass to this concept of God is basically because it seems to be a wholly irrelevant concept.

---

[9] With humble apologies to Douglas Adams.

I have even gone so far as to say that, while I am an atheist with regard to standard concepts of God, I would consider myself to be agnostic with regard to the Deist God, since there's neither evidence *for* nor evidence *against* a God who, by its very nature, does not interact with the universe in any way.

Well, that was then and this is now. After giving the matter a lot of thought, I'm finally ready to assert that I know that the Deist God does not exist to the same extent that I know that all other concepts of God do not exist (which is to say, as much as I can claim to know *anything* in life, including that I am a conscious being, that I only have one head on my shoulders, that the earth is round and rotates, etc.). Keep in mind, of course, that the following is not offered as any sort of "proof" that the Deist God does not exist, but simply to explain why I can feel confident that I know that it does not exist, to the same level of confidence that I claim to be able to know anything.

First of all, many modern Deists like to claim that Deism is wholly separate from the ancient superstitions that produced every other concept of God, whether it be the Sumerian gods, the ancient Greek and Roman gods, the Egyptian gods, the Norse gods, or even the God of the Bible. "Those gods are all based on ignorant superstition," they like to say, "but *our* concept of God is derived from wholly logical and rational considerations of the universe." Except, this claim is not actually supported by the history of modern Deism:

> *Deism gained prominence among intellectuals during the Age of Enlightenment, especially in Britain, France, Germany, and the United States. Typically, these had been raised as Christians and believed in one God, but they had become disenchanted with organized religion and orthodox teachings such as the Trinity, Biblical inerrancy, and the supernatural interpretation of events, such as miracles.*

— Wikipedia

In other words, Deism was clearly a *response* to the prevailing concepts of God that were rooted in ancient superstitions and not some sort of *de novo* theology that came up with the idea of God from first principles and careful consideration of the universe. Or, to put it yet another way, when Deists realized how untenable it was to assert belief in something for which there was no good evidence (and for which there was plenty of counter evidence), they decided to argue for an impersonal and undetectable creator God rather than abandoning their faith all together. As a result, if we can dismiss all the mainstream theist concepts of God as the product of ignorant superstitions, we can also dismiss the Deist God for exactly the same reason, despite all the pseudo-intellectual gloss that has been applied to the underlying concept over the years.

Second of all, since the Deist God — by definition — does not interact with the universe in any detectable way whatsoever, the **only** way in which Deists can claim to know that such a God exists in the first place is through various logical and philosophical arguments. And **every single one of those arguments is flawed**. Every single argument in favor of there being a Deist God is based in an *Argument from Ignorance* (or "God of the Gaps") fallacy. Whether it be the so-called *Teleological Argument* (a.k.a. the Argument from Design), the *Cosmological Argument*, the *Fine-Tuned Universe Argument*, or what have you, they all basically claim that since we [supposedly] cannot explain some facet of the universe, the only possible explanation is a supernatural creator who exists outside of time and space and is somehow able to interact with matter and energy despite not being composed of either. Aside from the fact that we actually *can* now explain many of the things that used to be inexplicable (the theory of Evolution by Natural Selection, for example, now perfectly explains the apparent design in the natural world), **the lack of an explanation cannot, in**

itself, be evidence of some other explanation for which there is no independent evidence.

There have been many, many refutations of the various Deist arguments for the existence of God over the years, many of which I have already covered earlier in this chapter, including the _God of the Gaps_ argument on p. 78, _A Response to the Argument from Design_ on p. 81, _A Response to the Cosmological Argument_ on p. 86 and _A Response to the "Fine-Tuned Universe" Argument_ on p. 96. To quote the late, great Christopher Hitchens, "That which can be asserted without evidence, can be dismissed without evidence." Deists acknowledge that there neither is nor can there be any direct observable evidence for the existence of their God, and all of their philosophical arguments are based on flawed premises that by necessity lead to incorrect conclusions.

Finally, even if the Deist God weren't rooted in the same ignorant superstitions as mainstream theist concepts of God, and even if the various Deist arguments weren't fatally flawed, the Deist God requires a belief in a logically impossible "supernatural" being of some sort that somehow exists "outside of space and time" and that is made of neither matter nor energy (yet is somehow able to interact with matter and energy at least with regard to creating both). Can I "prove" that nothing supernatural exists? No, but I assert that the term itself is meaningless and therefore I know (again, to the same degree that I claim to know anything) that the Deist God does not and cannot possibly exist. For more on this, see _Why the Word "Supernatural" Is Meaningless_) on p. 55 and _The Logical Impossibility of God_ on p. 150.

Of course, your mileage may vary, but this is what _I_ know to be true and why I feel confident saying that I know it to be true.

Analogies Are Not Arguments

Occasionally, a theist will offer up an analogy to show how we can know that God exists despite the lack of any evidence. These analogies usually look similar to the following:

> *"You can't see the air but you know that it's around. It's the same with God!"*

> *"You can't see electricity but you know that it exists because of the effect is has on the environment. It's the same with God!"*

The thing is, though, that these are not actually arguments and are instead just analogies. Analogies are wonderful things in that they make it easier to explain and understand complex subjects. But analogies don't actually prove anything or provide evidence of anything and are really only useful if both of the following are true:

1. The underlying concept the analogy is seeking to explain is actually a true concept to begin with.

2. The analogy is actually a *good* one, meaning that the comparison it makes is actually relevant.

The various "God" analogies described above fail for both of these reasons. First of all, they *assume* that God exists instead of offering any evidence to that effect and then expect the analogy to somehow convince people to accept that assumption. If you can't first demonstrate that God exists in the first place, using an analogy to explain why His existence can't be detected doesn't really get you very far.

Second of all, of course, they are simply bad analogies. For example, let's look at the "argument" that "you can't see the air but you know it's around" (presumably meant to prove that the same is true of God and the fact that we can't see Him doesn't mean He doesn't exist). Let's see how well our knowledge of air stacks up against theists' supposed knowledge of God:

We primarily know about air based on the writings of people who lived thousands of years ago, just like theists primarily know about God based on the writings of people who lived thousands of years ago. **Oh, wait — that's not true**.

We mostly know that air exists because people claimed to have actually seen it thousands of years ago, even though it's completely invisible today, just like people claimed to see and talk with God thousands of years ago even though nobody sees him today. **Oh, wait — that's not true**.

We have hundreds of different, often conflicting, descriptions today of what air actually is and how it acts, just like theists throughout the world and throughout history have hundreds (if not thousands) of different, often conflicting, descriptions of what God actually is and how He acts. **Oh, wait — that's not true**.

We are completely unable to detect air via any scientific instruments whatsoever and therefore have to accept its existence purely on faith, just like theists are completely unable to detect God via any scientific instruments and therefore have to accept His existence purely on faith. **Oh, wait — that's not true**.

Although we can occasionally detect the effect air has on the rest of the world, we can't do so in any sort of *consistent* manner since "air moves in mysterious ways." So, sometimes when we blow into a balloon it inflates, but other times it doesn't. And sometimes when we inhale the air fills our lungs, but other times it just refuses to enter. This is just like how theists are unable to *consistently* detect the effect God has on the rest of the world since "God moves in mysterious ways." So, sometimes He heals people who pray for healing, but other times He doesn't. It's exactly the same. **Oh, wait — that's not true**.

So, yeah. Not a particularly good analogy, sorry, and definitely not any sort of argument (valid, sound or otherwise).

Pascal's Wager

Pascal's famous wager is not so much an argument for the existence of God as it is an argument for why one should try to force oneself to believe in God. Pascal's argument can be paraphrased as follows:

> *Assuming there is a non-zero chance that God exists, and assuming that the reward for believing in God (if he exists) is eternal salvation, and assuming that the penalty for NOT believing in God (if he exists) is eternal damnation, and assuming that there is no downside to believing in God even if he doesn't exist, then the only logical course of action is to believe in God.*

Basically, I think that all of his assumptions are false, or at least not verifiably true. To wit:

Assuming there is a non-zero chance that God exists:

Why assume that there is a non-zero chance that God exists? Given the complete lack of empirical data to prove his existence, and given the many counterarguments to his existence (the existence of evil in the world, the fact that different people have claimed to receive conflicting messages from God, the fact that many so-called "miracles" have been proven to be the result of natural forces or merely delusions, etc.), maybe there is only a one in a million chance that God exists, or perhaps a one in a billion chance. Or, perhaps even a zero chance that God exists. Pascal's wager could just as likely be used to prove the rationality of believing that a flock of pink elephants will fly into my window one night and grant my heart's fondest desires. I mean, anything's possible, right?

Assuming that the reward for believing in God (if he exists) is eternal salvation:

What proof is there that believing in God will automatically result in eternal life, let alone eternal salvation? Different religions have different beliefs, and not all religions believe in an afterlife. Assuming there is a God of some sort, maybe he has simply created us as playthings and has no desire to let us return to his presence. Or maybe the whole purpose of life is to enjoy ourselves fully while we can, since the rest of eternity will be mind-numbing boredom as we sit on a cloud and strum a harp all day long.

Assuming that the penalty for NOT believing in God (if he exists) is eternal damnation:

Who is to say that the penalty for NOT believing is eternal damnation? Again, assuming there is a God of some sort, maybe He really doesn't care what we do here on earth. Claiming that all nonbelievers will have eternal torment and misery is pretty cruel and heartless when you think of all the BILLIONS of people who are raised in societies where a belief in God is not taught (not to mention all the BILLIONS of people who lived on the earth before the Bible was even written). God is the one who decides where and when somebody will be born, so why would he then condemn that person to Hell for never hearing about him?

Assuming that there is no downside to believing in God even if he doesn't exist:

Who's to say that there is no downside to believing in a non-existent God? Perhaps if you are a born again Christian who thinks that it is enough to simply "accept Jesus into your heart" to be saved, then this assumption is valid. The religion in which I was raised, however taught that God demands a life of self-sacrifice and obedience; no premarital sex, no alcohol, 10% of your income donated to the church, significant amounts of time devoted to performing various tasks (attending meetings, visiting other members, preparing lessons, performing sacred ordinances, etc.). If you believe that all of this is required of you to gain the promised reward and there ISN'T really a God, you will have essentially wasted your entire life to some degree or another. Economists call this "Opportunity Cost." This isn't to say there can't also be some benefits to trying to live a wholly religious life (maybe you get mutual support from other believers, maybe you have an easier time dealing with the death of a loved one, etc.), but these benefits don't erase the potential costs.

An additional downside to believing in a nonexistent god is the sacrifice of my capacity to rationally distinguish between what is real and what is fantasy. If I'm willing to believe in God simply because it's a "safe bet", then why not also believe in UFOs, psychics, ghosts, etc.? Maybe the UFOs will only rescue those who believe in them when the day of Armageddon is at hand. Or maybe the TV psychics can only convey messages from the loved ones of those who believe in psychic powers. Or maybe ghosts only visit those who are willing to see them? Forcing myself to believe in something for which there is no evidence and plenty of counter-evidence can only diminish my ability to think rationally.

Then the only logical course of action is to believe in God:

Basically, I think the argument boils down to "the theoretical reward is so great, and the cost to play is so minimal, that it is in your best interest to play." I suppose an analogy could be made, perhaps, to one of those multi-state lotteries where the prize has risen to $300 million and the chance of winning is 1 in 100 million. If the tickets are only $1 each, it only makes sense to play, since the potential gain is enormous and the potential loss is trivial.

However, I don't think that analogy is really accurate. For a closer analogy, you would be required to sell everything that you own in order to enter the lottery with the same 1 in 100 million chance of winning. Not only that, but there are 4000 different lotteries to choose from, and — at most — *one* of them will not be a scam (that is, only one can possibly be legitimate, but it's possible that they are all scams). Oh — and if you lose (which is likely), your whole life would be ruined as a result.

In conclusion

To sum up, since there is no way to tell if there is *any* chance that God exists, and since there is no guarantee that God would reward belief with eternal life if He did exist, and since there's no guarantee that God would reward disbelief with eternal damnation, and since the penalty for believing in a nonexistent God is potentially very high, the only logical thing is to not believe in God.

Ten Random Questions for Apologists

Although I have never personally engaged in a formal debate with a theistic apologist, I have had the chance to watch many recorded debates online. And each time I watch one of these debates, I can't help thinking of all the questions I would love to ask the person presenting the theistic side of the argument that neither the other debater nor the audience members thought to ask. Now, I'm not saying these are all unanswerable questions that would somehow "win" the debate (especially since two thousand years of formal apologetics have allowed modern theists to come up with some sort of answer to just about anything thrown their way) but I'd like to think they are questions which would, at the very least, indicate the weakness of some of the theistic positions and assertions and therefore should be asked.

And so, in no particular order:

1. Why do you keep asserting that the universe was "obviously" finely tuned to support life (and specifically intelligent human life), when 99.99999999... % of the known universe is utterly and completely hostile to the existence of life (let alone to human life)? Is all the rest of the vastness of space just for the sake of decoration?

2. You said that the observed suffering in the natural world is the direct result of mankind sinning in the Garden of Eden and causing the world (universe?) to enter into a "fallen state" with suffering and death. If God is both all-powerful and loving, however, why did he create a universe where man's sinning would affect all of creation and not just humanity? Why would God punish innocent animals instead of just punishing humanity?

3. You claimed that the creation of the universe "out of nothing" proves the existence of God, since there's no other possible explanation for something to come from nothing. Now that physicists have described ways in which a universe *could* have arisen out of nothing by purely natural processes (see, for example, *A Universe from Nothing* by theoretical physicist and cosmologist Lawrence M. Krauss) why does it matter whether physicists can prove that this is how it *actually* happened? Since you previously said God *must* exist because there was no other *possible* way it could have happened, isn't it a sufficient refutation of your "proof" that there is, in fact, at least one *possible* way after all?

4. As a Christian, what does it matter that some percentage (that you completely made up) of humanity throughout history has had some sort of spiritual experience that led them to believe in some sort of god or gods? Even if that somehow proved that there was *some* sort of god (which it

doesn't, since it would only prove at most that humans have a tendency to believe in supernatural beings), what justification is there for assuming that the "god" in question is the Christian one and not, say, the God of Islam, Zoroastrianism, Norse mythology, etc.?

5. How can you claim that the Bible is evidence of the existence of God and then admit that much of it is allegorical and not to be taken literally? Especially when, once upon a time, it was *all* thought to be literally true until science and evolving societal norms slowly but surely proved that more and more of it couldn't *possibly* be literally true? Also, how do you determine which parts are literally true and which parts are merely allegorical? Does it bother you that the determination of which parts are literal and which parts are allegorical has changed over time, indicating that there is no "correct" answer other than "everything is literally true that hasn't yet been shown to be demonstrably false or distasteful to our modern sensibilities"?

6. On a related note, how can you claim that "absolute morality" can only come from God and then acknowledge that the only source we have for what God's morality actually is (*i.e.*, the Bible) contains numerous laws and principles that do not apply to today's society and therefore are not absolute?

7. You claimed that God is necessary in order to explain what the purpose of life is, which is something science cannot do. What justification do you have for the assertion that life *must* necessarily have a purpose in the first place, other than the fact that you find the notion of a life without a purpose to be too depressing to contemplate?

8. Once you have "logically proven" the necessity of some sort of timeless and immaterial supernatural being in order to

explain the creation of the universe and all its laws (leaving aside for the moment the question as to whether you actually did prove anything), how do you get from that supernatural being to the God of your particular religion and your particular sect of your particular religion? If you're trying to prove something, it's not enough to just say you have faith in your God or that your God personally spoke to your heart. You're perfectly entitled to your faith, but that's not the "proof" you promised to provide.

9. If it is possible to infer the existence of a "designer" from the complexity observed throughout the natural world, why is it not therefore also possible to infer that this "designer" must be incompetent, sadistic and/or merely a non-sentient natural process from the existence of all the many, many design flaws observed in nature (cancers, genetic diseases, age-related decrepitude, parasitical infections, viruses, etc.)?

10. If God really *meant* that he would answer all sincere prayers, but sometimes the answer will be "no" (which is the standard explanation for why faithful Christians don't always get what they ask for), then why does the Bible say over and over again[10] that God promises to actually *give* his faithful followers "whatsoever" they ask for in his name?

---

[10] For example, "*Therefore I say unto you, what things soever ye desire, when ye pray, believe that ye receive them, and ye shall have them* (Mark 11:24)" or, "*And all things, whatsoever ye shall ask in prayer, believing, ye shall receive* (Matthew 21:22)" or, "And whatsoever ye shall ask in my name, that will I do, that the Father may be glorified in the Son (John 14:13)" or, "*And whatsoever we ask, we receive of him, because we keep his commandments, and do those things that are pleasing in his sight* (1 John 3:22)."

Feel free to raise any or all of these questions if you ever find yourself involved in a debate (whether in-person or online). Again, they likely won't cause you to "win" the debate, but you never know. At the very least, you might make some of the audience members reconsider their positions a bit.

Chapter 9.   Arguments for the Non-Existence of God

The previous chapter offered counter-arguments to some of the most common arguments offered for the existence of a god of some sort of another. In this chapter, on the other hand, I present some possible affirmative arguments for the non-existence of God (specifically the so-called Abrahamic God of the Bible and the Qur'an) that go beyond merely refuting arguments that supposedly prove that God exists.

Why It's Obvious that Gods Do Not Exist

Throughout this book I provide many different arguments and explanations and answers for why it's just common sense to reject claims about the existence of gods, but they all boil down to the same three basic points:

1. **The claim that any gods exist is a truly extraordinary claim completely divorced from normal human experience.**

   As such, the default position *should* be to reject such a claim unless and until some evidence is provided to support that claim, as with any other extraordinary claims such as the existence of magic, alien abductions, fairies, etc. In addition, the extraordinary nature of these claims means that extraordinary evidence should be required to overcome that default position, beyond such ambiguous things like anecdotal stories, personal feelings, unverified "miracles" or claims that science cannot currently explain some aspects of the natural world and therefore "God did it" must be the only possible explanation.

2. **The evidence that *should* be there if any of the gods actually worshiped by anybody really existed is not there.**

Yes, you can argue the possibility of some sort of "hidden" or "undetectable" deity of some sort that we can never know anything about because it either exists "outside of time and space" or resides in some far corner of the universe we can never explore or is some sort of immaterial "pure spirit" that cannot be detected by any scientific means or whatever. But, aside from the fact that there is literally no justifiable reason to believe in any such "hidden" deity in the first place apart from wishful thinking, the various gods actually worshiped by anybody throughout history have all been described as interacting with humanity and saying and doing and promising to do very specific things for which there should be plenty of very obvious evidence. Despite whatever aphorisms you may have read or heard on the subject, absence of evidence really *is* evidence of absence when there *should* be evidence.

3. **We know the origin of beliefs in gods.**

The belief in just about every deity actually worshiped throughout human history can be traced to very specific origins in ancient books filled with superstition and obviously the product of ignorant people who were trying to invent explanations for life's so-called "big questions" such as "Where did we come from," "Why are we here" and "What happens to us after we die." Just about every culture we know about has come up with its own [mostly] unique "creation story" populated by one or more supernatural beings to answer these questions. And, as a result, there is no good reason to suspect that one of those many stories invented by one small (at the time) section of the world's population is actually the truth.

The Problem of Evil

One of the most compelling arguments against the existence of God (or, at least, the sort of all powerful, all knowing and all benevolent God worshiped by most religions) is the so-called "Problem of Evil". Stated simply, it asks how a God who is supposed to be an all knowing, all powerful and all loving being could allow so much suffering to occur. The ancient Greek philosopher Epicurus is said to have put it this way:

Is God willing to prevent evil, but not able? Then he is not omnipotent. Is he able, but not willing? Then he is malevolent. Is he both able and willing? Then whence cometh evil? Is he neither able nor willing? Then why call him God?

There seem to be two standard responses to this argument that are made by theists, each of which I will address below:

1. God gave mankind free will, and if one person wants to do harm to another person then God cannot prevent that from happening without taking away that free will. In other words, God could prevent suffering, but that would cause something even worse to occur (the loss of our free will).

2. Adam and Eve's transgression in the Garden of Eden caused the entire world to become a cursed place, full of pain and suffering. The "fall" from God's grace affected all of creation, and all of creation therefore suffers as a result of man's sin.

The first response to the problem of evil is actually a fairly persuasive argument for why God permits suffering that is actually caused by other people (or even caused by people themselves). Yes, free will is a wonderful thing and it would be pretty bad if we were all just a bunch of mindless robots forced to act the way God wants us to act.

However, this argument says precisely **nothing** about why people suffer as the result of natural causes such as diseases, famine, blizzards, droughts, earthquakes, tsunamis, etc., none of which are the result of man's exercising his free will. OK, sure, I suppose an argument could be made that some of what we call "natural causes" do, in fact, have some basis in man's exercise of free will. Perhaps you could argue that some people get lung cancer, say, because of the choice they made to smoke cigarettes. Or that some people needlessly die in hurricanes because we as a species have largely chosen to ignore the evidence of anthropogenic climate change. I would argue, however, that those cases are few and far between when compared with all the other forms of suffering that clearly have nothing to do with our free will, unless you want to get completely reductive and claim that, since person X chose to live in a part of the world where tornadoes occasionally happen, it's his fault that he (and his family, of course) are later killed by a tornado.

Moreover, this free will argument does not address why there is so much suffering in the rest of the world. Sure, you can blame man's free will for some of the suffering (deforestation, pollution, etc.), but man's free will can't be blamed for the fact that the majority of animal life either need to feed on other animals in order to survive or get eaten by other animals. It doesn't explain why animals also get painful, debilitating diseases. It doesn't explain why there are species of wasps that lay their eggs in the bodies of living creatures that die a slow and agonizing death as the wasp larvae hatch and eat their way out.

So, yeah – free will is important and can explain man's inhumanity to man. Aside from that, though, it's not a particularly compelling argument.

The second response to the problem of evil has many flaws, but the primary one in my opinion is that it apparently takes away God's free will and/or renders him powerless. It's basically saying that God didn't want all of creation to suffer but had no choice due to Adam's transgression. Really? He had no choice? Let's think about that for a minute, shall we? If God is all powerful, surely He could have come up with a way to punish Adam (and all of his descendants) without punishing every other living thing on the planet (and perhaps even the universe). Either God had no choice in the matter in which case He is not all powerful after all, or else He chose to inflict as much suffering as possible on all of His creation, in which case He is not all loving.

I suppose one could argue that God really only cares about humans and just isn't concerned with the suffering of lesser creatures who (presumably) have no souls and just exist to make the world a more colorful place. That doesn't seem to match the biblical description of God as a being who cares about a single sparrow falling to the ground, however.

Again, this argument assumes that it's man's fault that the world fell from grace into a state of suffering, but that's only valid if you also assume that God was powerless or unwilling to prevent it from happening, or at least from happening in the way that it did. If God really wanted to punish man for Adam's sin (and I'll leave the morality of punishing people for a sin committed by a distant ancestor for another post), wouldn't it have been more effective to make man suffer and die while simultaneously leaving the rest of creation in an Edenic state as a constant reminder of what was lost?

The bottom line is that, if God actually exists and is a being as described in holy scriptures, He is the one who set up the whole system in the first place. He is the one who decided what the punishment would be for the transgressions of Adam. Claiming it is Adam's fault for causing the world to enter a "fallen" state due to his sin is like a having a dictator prescribe genocide for sneezing and then blaming somebody who sneezes for the fact that the dictator was "forced" to wipe out an entire village as a result.

Which is Easier to Believe, that Life Was created by God or by Chance?

OK, this question gets asked a *lot* by theists in a lot of different ways. At its core, it's simply a form of the classic "Argument from Design" that I addressed previously. But let's look at this from a slightly different perspective, shall we?

Time and again, we see theists claiming that it is just too *improbable* or *inconceivable* to imagine that life could have originated "by chance" and therefore the most reasonable explanation is that it was created by the omnipotent, omniscient, all-loving and perfect God described by the particular religion of which they happen to be a member.

Unfortunately for theists, the life we see on earth is far from what we would actually *expect* to see if it were actually created by an omnipotent, omniscient, all-loving and perfect God, the way we would expect to see a finely crafted watch from a master watchmaker. Instead of perfection and fine craftsmanship, we see eyes that have blind spots, vestigial organs that occasionally burst open and kill us, cells that periodically start reproducing uncontrollably (cancer), a propensity for genetic flaws that cause all sorts of diseases such as Downs Syndrome and Tay-Sachs disease, a whole system that gradually breaks down as you get older, etc., etc., etc. So much for "fine craftsmanship," eh?

And that's just the human condition! Sure, it's pretty amazing that plants and animals so closely depend on each other for survival and it's so cool that bees are attracted to beautiful flowers who need the bees to spread their pollen. What a great design! How perfect! But then you also have the fact that there are parasites that have to lay their eggs in living hosts so their larva can hatch and eat their way out to survive. Not quite so beautiful and perfect. And then there's the whole predator/pray relationship where some animals have to brutally kill other animals to survive (and the prey animals have to be brutally killed in order to not overpopulate and starve to death). And don't forget that the rest of the animal kingdom also gets nasty diseases and suffer accidents and experience pain and agony.

As a result, theists find themselves in the position of coming up with a whole bunch of additional justifications and rationalizations as to why life is so flawed when it was supposedly created by a perfect being, including one or more of the following:

- *All of nature used to be perfect before Adam sinned and caused the entire universe to enter a fallen state. Which means, what, God is a sadistic bastard who set up a system whereby ALL OF NATURE would need to suffer for the sins of one person instead of just punishing that one person?*

- *God specifically gave us these flawed bodies to provide us with obstacles in life to be overcome or to test our faith or some other reason known only to him because he works in mysterious ways. And I guess all those cute, furry animals that die horrible agonizing deaths also have important lessons to learn as well, huh?*

- *It doesn't matter whether life is flawed right now, since life is but a twinkling of an eye compared to all eternity and we'll all have perfect bodies in the next life.*

- *"You are assuming the human body can be better designed under these circumstances. Maybe it can't. You are also assuming it is not a work in progress. You can probably imagine the first watches were not fine-tuned machines." (An actual response I received from a theist, who apparently thinks an omnipotent, omniscient, all-loving and perfect being needs theists like him to make excuses for His shoddy workmanship and who doesn't understand what "omnipotent" actually means.)*

It doesn't matter what your personal favorite justification is. The point is that, despite what theists claim, the evidence of our senses does not automatically give us reason to believe in the sort of God that most theists claim to believe in (omnipotent, omniscient, all-loving and perfect) and theists MUST tack on other conditions for which there is no evidence.

Naturalism (or "atheism", if you insist), on the other hand, requires no such additional caveats and conditions and justifications to be believable. We know from observation that there are natural laws that govern how the universe works. And, although we may not have perfect knowledge of every natural law, there is no reason not to believe that those laws can explain every single observed phenomenon, including the origin of life itself.

- So, which is easier to believe? That the natural world evolved to be the way it is — warts and all — due to purely the natural processes that govern the universe, or that the natural world was designed by an omnipotent, omniscient, all-loving and perfect God who, for some reason we can't quite figure out, decided to make the world *look* as if it had evolved to be the way it is — warts and all — due to purely the natural processes that govern the universe? My money is on the former.

One final thought. To many theists, there are only two options — either life was created "by God" or else it happened "by chance." And "by chance" apparently means completely randomly, entirely by coincidence, etc. This is a false dichotomy, however. "By chance" in this context simply means without being directed by any sort of intelligence, yet still according to natural laws that guide and constrain the outcome.

Doesn't the Beauty and Majesty of the Natural World Prove that God Exists?

A question that gets frequently asked of atheists is how we can possibly look at all the wonders of the natural world and **not** believe in God? Now, sure, this is partially just a restatement of the classic "Argument from Design" that I addressed previously and it also involves a fair amount of arguing from ignorance or incredulity ("I can't personally imagine how such a thing is possible without God, therefore it must not be possible"). But I think it actually goes a little deeper than that.

After all, once upon a time, we really *did* have no idea what caused sunsets, how mountains formed, how rock structures came to looked like they were carved into interesting shapes, etc., so it only made sense to think that such things were specifically created for our benefit. But now we obviously are able to explain how all these things are caused by purely natural forces and principles, so this question can't just be due to sheer ignorance of how the natural world works. There must be more to it than that.

But hey — maybe this all just means that God created all the natural laws in the first place and therefore is ultimately responsible for it turning out the way it has. Sure, God didn't *personally* sculpt the amazing rock formations seen in Utah's Zion National Park or the Grand Canyon, but can't we still give Him the credit for creating the rocks and wind and water and setting up a natural system whereby rocks can be eroded by wind and water? And sure, maybe God doesn't *personally* paint every single beautiful sunset by hand, but we can still praise Him for creating the water cycles that causes clouds to form and making it so that sunlight refracts when it strikes water droplets, etc., right? And, OK, so maybe God didn't *personally* cause those majestic mountains to rise out of the crust and get covered with snow, but we can still worship Him for coming up with the idea of plate tectonics and snow in the first place, right? After all, God created the entire universe from scratch, and therefore every beautiful and awesome and great thing we see in that universe must therefore be the result of God's will, right?

So, maybe the argument is not simply about how could all these things exist without God but instead why would they all be so majestic and beautiful and awe-inspiring without God. Surely God must have set things up so that the end results would be so amazing, right?

OK, let's play that game. The natural world is full of amazing, beautiful, wonderful and awe-inspiring things that prove that God exists and loves us enough to share all this beauty with us. Gotcha. Now let's take a look at all the things in the natural world that *aren't* so great, shall we? Let's look at the volcanic eruptions instead of just looking at the majestic mountains. Let's look at the vast dust storms instead of just looking at the pretty sunsets. Let's look at the floods and earthquakes and droughts and lightning strikes and tornadoes and hurricanes and tsunamis instead of just looking at the amazing rock formations. And then go look at the children dying of genetic diseases and the ugliness of things like Ebola and smallpox and parasitic infections and flesh-eating bacteria. Care to look at some picture of people with half of their face eaten off? Seriously — go ahead and do a Google image search for flesh-eating bacteria. It's OK, I'll wait for you to finish vomiting at the sight and come back here.

.

.

.

Still with me? Wonderful. Now, after looking at all that ugliness in the world, you go ahead and tell me that it's all a testament to just how depraved and sadistic and cruel God is, since He created the universe from scratch and therefore every horrible and ugly and terrible thing we see in that universe must also be the result of God's will.

No, you can't claim that the ugliness is just random stuff not under God's direct control or all the work of Satan.

No, you can't claim that all the bad stuff is the result of man's exercise of free will, since I didn't even mention anything related to man's inhumanity to man.

No, you can't claim that Adam and Eve sinned and somehow caused the entire universe to enter a "fallen" state since (a) that would mean that a supposedly loving God decided to punish the entire universe for the sins of two people and (b) it would also negate all the previously "great" things that you previously gave God credit for. I mean, seriously — either the world is full of ugliness because it is in a fallen state or else it is full of beauty and greatness because of God. You can't have it both ways.

So, please. Go ahead. You admit that all the ugliness in the world is evidence that God is a sadistic bastard (or, perhaps doesn't exist at all), and I'll admit that the beauty in the natural world is evidence that He does exist and loves us so much that He wants to share His glory with us. You don't get to just look at the good and ignore the bad and claim that it somehow proves something.

Having said all that, let me just make it clear that I *do* think there are many beautiful, majestic and awe-inspiring sights in the natural world, both here on earth and out in the rest of the known universe. And no, I don't think the entire universe is a dark and depressing place just because there are also many ugly, hideous and scary things as well. I take the good with the bad and understand that this is what happens when you have a universe that operates on impersonal natural principles and that wasn't designed specifically for our benefit.

The Logical Impossibility of God

Is God constrained by the laws of logic? It's an important question, and the answer seems to be, "Yes, but only when it's convenient to say that He is."

It's an old chestnut of a question, but whenever theists start talking about how their particular version of God is "omnipotent" some atheist wag will invariably ask, "If God is omnipotent, can He create a stone so massive that He can't move it?" To which the theist will usually respond, "that's a logical impossibility and being omnipotent means being able to do anything **logically** possible." OK, so no creating a stone too massive for Him to move, no creating a square circle, no acting against His own nature, etc. Got it. And, presumably, this is because logic transcends human understanding and provides general principles of existence. There isn't "human logic" and "God's logic," there's just *logic*.

With me so far?

OK, now one of the fundamental principles of logic is the so-called "Law of Non-contradiction," which in its basic form states that, "Contradictory statements cannot both be true in the same sense at the same time." This means that the two propositions "A is B" and "A is not B" are mutually exclusive. It also means that something cannot simultaneously be two opposite things. This is why, for example, there can be no such thing as a square circle or a married bachelor since both concepts involve a self-contradiction.

So, is there anything about God's supposed nature that violates the Law of Non-contradiction and would therefore make God logically impossible?

Well, one place to start would be to examine the relationship between him supposedly being both omnipotent (all powerful) and omnibenevolent (all loving). This leads to the famous "Problem of Evil" that I discussed in the previous chapter which unequivocally proves the logical impossibility of God since (a) Evil cannot exist if there is an omnipotent, omnibenevolent God and (b) we know from our own experience that there is, in fact, evil.

Well, not quite...

Although this argument has been sufficient to convince many people throughout history to reject the idea of God (or at least the all-loving and omnipotent God of Christianity), those who cling to their beliefs have come up with numerous ways to get around the apparent contradiction:

> "Evil is the result of human free will and, since God values free will more than anything, He allows evil."

Except, of course, this only applies to evil acts done as a result of human free will (murder, rape, robbery, etc.) and wholly ignores things like pain and suffering caused by genetic diseases, natural disasters, accidents, etc.

> "When Adam and Eve sinned against God in the Garden of Eden, the world fell into a fallen state, so all the evils in the world are a direct result of those actions."

Except, of course, this doesn't explain why God would need to punish the entire world (not to mention universe) because of the actions of two people. Why not simply punish Adam and Eve (and all their descendants if God were feeling particularly vengeful) and leave the rest of the natural world alone? Why make animals die horribly painful and cruel deaths just to teach us a lesson? Wouldn't it be a more powerful lesson if everything in nature was blissfully happy except for us? Besides, God is the one who set the whole system up in the first place, so it was his decision to make the whole universe suffer for the sins of Adam and Eve and not their free will.

"This life is a test, and how we deal with suffering will determine our eternal fate."

Well, OK, but that seems awfully callous when applying it to, say, young children who are born with horrible genetic diseases that cause them to lead painfully short lives. It also doesn't address all the pain and suffering throughout the rest of the natural world.

And the list goes on and on. The bottom line is that there's always some way to define "omnipotent", "omnibenevolent" and even "evil" to avoid inherent contradictions, even if the newly defined terms don't really make much sense or accord with experience. "An all-loving God is one who lets His children have free will, not freedom from suffering." "Pain and suffering are actually good things, not evils." You get the idea. As I said, a lot of people are not convinced by these rationalizations, but they do make it hard to state unequivocally that God is logically impossible solely due to the so-called Problem of Evil.

OK, how about this? In order to create the universe, which is the totality of all time and space and matter and energy, God must exist outside of time and space and not be composed of matter or energy. But if God exists outside time, then how could He have ever chosen the moment to create the universe in the first place? After all, the idea that first the universe didn't exist and then it did exist implies the occurrence of a sequence of events, which is what time is. So, a "timeless" God who performs an act that requires time is definitely a logical impossibility, right?

Well, what do you know? That actually *is* a logical impossibility, and the only response theists have is to claim that "existing outside of time" means something other than actually existing outside of time. God experiences all time at once, for example. Or time means something different to God, and we poor humans are just too dense to understand it. So, yeah, once again they are able to weasel out of the logical impossibility of God by redefining terms.

OK, but if God is not composed of matter or energy, how can He possibly have created matter and energy in the first place and how can He continue to interact with it today? That seems like a logical contradiction for sure, doesn't it?

Well, once again, not *quite*...

Even if we accept that God is composed of neither matter nor energy, we cannot state unequivocally that He would therefore be unable to interact with matter and energy. In the same way that energy can interact with matter despite not being composed of matter, God *could* be composed of some entirely different substance (let's call it "mind" or "spirit") that can interact with matter and energy in some way we have never observed and just can't understand. Of course, we now know that energy actually is composed of matter in a very real sense, but that just means the analogy (commonly used by theistic apologists) is a bad one. It doesn't change the fact that God logically *could* be composed of some other substance that allows Him to interact with matter and energy without being composed of matter or energy Himself. Hey, maybe it's that "dark matter" or "dark energy" that scientists are always talking about! Yeah, that sounds nice and science-y, so why not just go with that...

OK, so the mere fact that God somehow interacts with matter and energy
while being composed of neither is not, in and of itself, a logical impossibility. I think we are getting very close, however. You see, in

order to avoid any *apparent* contradictions inherent in the notion of a God who is timeless and not composed of matter or energy, Christian apologists over the years have declared that God is both "Transcendent" and "Immanent". According to Wikipedia, the two terms are defined as follows:

> **Transcendence** *refers to the aspect of a god's nature and power which is wholly independent of the material universe, beyond all physical laws. This is contrasted with* **Immanence**, *where a god is said to be fully present in the physical world and thus accessible to creatures in various ways.*

Or, in other words, God is both wholly **apart** from the material universe and wholly **within** the material universe. At the same time. He is simultaneously **B** and **not B**. His very nature is therefore in violation of the Law of Non-contradiction and He is therefore logically impossible. Q.E.D.

Now, some will argue (and believe me, they have) that it doesn't matter if God is logically impossible since we're only talking about *human* logic here and God is above such things. Well, fine, except then why do you claim that an omnipotent God can't create a rock too massive for Him to move or can't create a square circle? Aren't those just principles of human logic as well? It seems that if you want to apply *some* logical principles to God, you would have to apply all of them (not just the ones that are convenient).

It seems that theists are left with three possible responses to this:

First, they can claim that God isn't bound by anything whatsoever and therefore *can* actually create a rock too massive for Him to move, create a square circle, etc. Of course, once you throw all logic out the window it becomes rather pointless to discuss anything, but some theists are apparently willing to do just this.

Second, they can claim that Immanence and Transcendence aren't actually opposites despite the plain definitions of the words. But, since the whole idea of God being both Immanent and Transcendent is a way to explain how He could create the universe and still be part of the universe, there's no real way of getting around the fact that they are, in fact, complete opposites. A lot of theists do go down this path, but they are usually the same ones who will write dissertations on how God can simultaneously be three distinct beings and one unified being that is absolutely not made up of three distinct beings whatsoever [*"We worship one God in trinity, and trinity in unity, neither confounding the persons nor dividing the substance. For the person of the Father is one; of the Son, another; of the Holy Spirit, another. But the divinity of the Father and of the Son and of the Holy Spirit is one, the glory equal, the majesty equal. Such as is the Father, such also is the Son, and such the Holy Spirit. The Father is uncreated, the Son is uncreated, the Holy Spirit is uncreated. The Father is infinite, the Son is infinite, the Holy Spirit is infinite. The Father is eternal, the Son is eternal, the Holy Spirit is eternal. And yet there are not three eternal Beings, but one eternal Being. So also there are not three uncreated Beings, nor three infinite Beings, but one uncreated and one infinite Being. In like manner, the Father is omnipotent, the Son is omnipotent, and the Holy Spirit is omnipotent. And yet there are not three omnipotent Beings, but one omnipotent Being. Thus the Father is God, the Son is God, and the Holy Spirit is God. And yet there are not three Gods, but one God only. The Father is Lord, the Son is Lord, and the Holy Spirit is Lord. And yet there are not three Lords, but one Lord only. For as we are compelled by Christian truth to confess each person distinctively to be both God and Lord, we are prohibited by the Catholic religion to say that there are three Gods or Lords. The Father is made by none, nor created, nor begotten. The Son is from the Father alone, not made, not created, but begotten. The Holy Spirit is not created by the Father and the Son, nor begotten, but proceeds. Therefore, there is one Father, not three Fathers; one Son, not three Sons; one Holy Spirit, not three Holy Spirits. And in this Trinity there is nothing prior or posterior, nothing greater or less, but all three persons are coeternal and coequal to themselves. So that through all, as was said above, both unity in trinity and trinity in unity is to be adored. Whoever would be saved, let him thus think concerning the Trinity." –* The Athanasian Creed]

Finally, they can just wave their magical "Wand of Definitions" and state that God is defined as the sort of being who can be both Transcendent and Immanent without there being any sort of logical contradiction involved. Or that God really *is* above so-called "human" logic after all (meaning that He really *can* make a stone so massive that He can't move it, create a square circle and even act against His own nature). At which point it's rather hard to even continue the conversation since they obviously don't understand what a logical impossibility is.

The bottom line, as far as I am concerned, is that God is absolutely and undeniably logically impossible, a self-contradiction (at least as commonly depicted and worshiped). The only question is whether theists actually *care* about this fact or whether cognitive dissonance will force them to compartmentalize and ignore it so as to not feel any angst about their beliefs.

Debunking God and Religion in One Sentence

Somebody once challenged me online to provide in a single sentence the most powerful argument that belief in God and religion is nonsense. I honestly don't know if the person asking the question was a theist or an atheist or something in-between, but I had to laugh at the artificial stricture placed on any answers. One sentence? Why just one sentence instead of, say, a well-reasoned paragraph or two that might allow one to flesh out the argument a bit instead of just providing an easily dismissed sound bite?

[To be honest, I suspected the reason for the restriction was specifically so it *could* be easily refuted, but I suppose it could have just been because they wanted something pithy that didn't need a long-winded explanation.]

Anyway, there were certainly lots of ways to approach this question. I could, for example, mention the sheer number of religions in the world and the fact that so many of them are mutually exclusive. I could discuss the lack of any compelling evidence or sound arguments to support a belief in God. But, since the question specifically asked for an argument that belief in God and religion is "nonsense" (and not just improbable or irrational), I finally decided to go with the following:

> *The original concepts of gods and religions were the product of ignorant and superstitious people who had little or no understanding about the world or the universe and our place in it, and just about everything else they thought they knew to be true has now been proved to be false.*

Yeah, it's a bit clunky, but that's what you get when you ask somebody to cram an entire argument into a single sentence. Overall, though, I'm satisfied with the way it came out and I think it makes a valid point.

Of course, as expected, people immediately began taking cheap pot shots at my answer, demanding that I provide "citations" to "scientific evidence" to support my assertion that the people who first invented religions were largely ignorant about the world and the universe. Seriously? I need to prove that people living thousands of years ago, without access to any of the technology we have today, didn't know as much about the universe as we do today?

Well, I don't know about any "scientific evidence" of their ignorance that I can cite, but fortunately there's this wonderful invention that actually allows me to see backwards through time and know what ancient people were thinking when first describing their gods and coming up with their religions, as well as what they thought about the universe and our place in it. And it's an invention that has actually been around for many thousands of years.

It's called *writing*.

You see, we don't need "scientific evidence" to determine what ancient people were thinking when they first came up with their religions since they were nice enough to write it all down for us. From the ancient Sumerians who chiseled cuneiform stories into clay tablets, to the people who wrote the Bible, to the writings of the ancient Egyptians, Greeks and Romans, to the author(s) of the Qur'an, to the recorded Edda sagas of the ancient Norse, etc., we have an abundant treasure trove of literature that clearly indicates that the people first writing about gods and religions largely didn't have a clue about such basic things as the fact that the earth rotates on an axis, that the earth revolves around the sun, that the stars are actually other suns unimaginably far away and not, say, pinholes in the curtain of the night, that the universe is many billions of years old, that all life on earth evolved from earlier forms of life, that diseases are caused by germs, etc., etc., etc.

Add to that all the many, many, many different "creation stories" we have from all the various world religions and you don't need "scientific evidence" to understand that religions and gods were all invented by people with limited knowledge about, well, much of anything, really. Not that they were necessarily stupid or unsophisticated, of course, but simply *unaware* of things that could only be known with the help of tools such as telescopes, microscopes, rockets, computers, etc.

And please, don't start pointing out how one particular passage in one particular religion's holy book can, if translated and interpreted in just the right way, supposedly indicates that the author may have actually understood something about the world that most ignorant people at the time it was written probably didn't know. Especially if you are then going to completely ignore all the other passages that are obviously just plain wrong no matter how you squint your eyes at them. Seriously, don't tell me that "Let there Be Light" is an amazingly accurate scientific description of the Big Bang and then try to explain why it doesn't matter that the Bible also says the Earth was created before the Sun.

Goldberg's Razor™ and Logical Proofs for the Non-Existence of God [11]

Just about everybody has heard of the famous **Occam's Razor**™ (named after 13th century philosopher and theologian William of Ockham) that has come to mean "the simplest explanation is generally the correct one," but which was originally formulated as follows:

"Entities should not be multiplied without necessity."

A "razor" in this sense simply means a logical principle (not a law) that can help you decide between two competing hypotheses by cutting them apart and seeing which one is more likely, and Occam's Razor teaches us that the hypothesis that requires the fewest assumptions is most likely the one that is correct. With regard to religious beliefs, some people incorrectly think that Occam's Razor can best be applied by saying that "God did it" is the

---

[11] Please note that my use of the ™ symbol is meant to be humorous in nature. I have no idea if I am the first person to ever come up with this particular expression of this particular idea, but I definitely came up with it on my own and didn't copy it from anybody else. And in the same vein, none of the other razors I quote here are actually trademarked either.

simplest explanation for anything, since you don't need to make any other assumptions apart from God to explain it. A better use of Occam's Razor, however, would be to point that saying "God did it" actually *adds* an extra assumption to any natural explanation and that it requires even *more* assumptions to explain such things as how God actually "did it" and where God came from in the first place.

Many of you may also be familiar with the so-called **Sagan Standard**™ (named after famous astronomer and cosmologist Carl Sagan) which is another logical "razor" that states:

"Extraordinary claims require extraordinary evidence."

It essentially means that the further a claim is from our ordinary experience, the stronger the burden of proof is for those who make such a claim. When applied to religious matters, claims don't get much more extraordinary than the claim that there exists an intelligent being composed of "pure spirit" (whatever the heck that means) which exists "outside of time and space" (whatever the heck that means) while somehow still being capable of interacting with the material world and that purportedly cares deeply about every individual member of one particular species living on one particular world orbiting one particular star among billions in one particular galaxy among countless trillions of similar galaxies in this entire vast universe. And, therefore, the evidence required to establish such a claim needs to go well beyond things such as anecdotal stories, unverifiable claims of miracles, personal feelings, etc.

A much smaller group of people (mostly atheists) may also be familiar with **Hitchen's Razor**™ (named after famous atheist Christopher Hitchens) that states:

"What can be asserted without evidence can also be dismissed without evidence."

It essentially means that the burden of proof regarding the truthfulness of a claim always lies with the one who makes the claim, and if the person making the claim cannot meet their burden then the claim is unfounded and their opponent need not argue further in order to dismiss it. And with regard to religious discussions, it means that if somebody has provided no evidence or arguments to support their claims that a god exists, then there is no need for anybody to ever bother to try and refute those claims since they are wholly without merit to begin with.

Well, allow me to formally introduce what I'm going to call **Goldberg's Razor**™, which is something I have said many times in the past whenever somebody tries to prove the existence of God based on carefully chosen definitions of what the concept "God" means:

> **"That which can be defined into existence can just as easily be defined out of existence."**

It essentially means that if it's possible to prove the existence of something based solely on carefully chosen definitions (e.g., God exists because God is defined as a "necessarily existing being" or God exists because God is defined as "that which caused the universe to exist") without any actual empirical evidence to justify those definitions, then it is just as possible to prove the non-existence of that thing by using different, equally carefully chosen, definitions. For example, the following are all perfectly valid logical proofs of the *non-existence* of God that, like the aforementioned logical proofs for the *existence* of God, only work if you define your terms in such a way to require the conclusion (but which don't actually prove anything at all since those definitions do not necessarily reflect empirical reality):

Proof for the Non-Existence of God #1:

1. In order for God to have created the universe, He must exist outside the universe.

2. Anything that exists outside the universe cannot be said to exist within the universe.

3. The universe is defined as the totality of all existence, meaning that nothing can be said to exist if it is not inside the universe.

4. Therefore, God does not exist. Q.E.D.

Proof for the Non-Existence of God #2:

1. In order for anything to be said to exist, it must exist within time and within space.

2. God, however, is defined as being outside of time and space.

3. Therefore, God does not exist. Q.E.D.

Proof for the Non-Existence of God #3:

1. God is all-powerful, all-knowing and loving.

2. A loving being who is all-powerful and all-knowing would not allow the entire natural world to suffer caused by things beyond the control of the entities suffering (natural disasters, genetic diseases, cancers, parasitical infections, etc.).

3. The entire natural world, however, is filled with all sorts of suffering caused by things beyond the control of the entities suffering.

4. Therefore, God does not exist. Q.E.D.

Proof for the Non-Existence of God #4:

1. God is a being greater than which none can be imagined.

2. It is always possible to imagine a greater version of anything that actually exists in reality.

3. Anything that exists solely in the imagination cannot be said to exist in reality.

4. Therefore, God does not exist. Q.E.D.

Proof for the Non-Existence of God #5:

1. God is described in various holy books as a being who has said and done and promised to do very specific things for which there *should* be discoverable evidence if true.

2. None of the evidence that *should* be discoverable if God had actually said and done and promised to do what he is described as having said and done and promised to do has ever been discovered, despite thousands of years of people attempting to find such evidence.

3. Therefore, the God described in various holy books does not actually exist.

And remember – I am not claiming that any of these arguments *actually* prove the non-existence of God (although they should certainly make some people at least reconsider their position). Logical arguments are only as good as their premises and definitions, and they can be used to supposedly "prove" anything if you choose your definitions carefully and assert the desired premises. Every single logical argument for the *existence* of God is flawed because they include arbitrary definitions and/or asserted premises that are not necessarily true in all cases. And the examples I have provided are simply meant to point that out by showing that it's just as easy to use similar arguments to prove the *non*-existence of God.

Chapter 10.   Musings on Morality

Many theists like to use morality as a way of attacking atheists, either to claim that atheists cannot possibly be moral without a belief in a god of some sort or to claim that existence of "objective" morality proves the existence of a god of some sort because a god is the only possible source of such morality. In the following essays I explore these claims and discuss where morality actually comes from, what role religion plays, and whether or not it even makes sense to talk about "objective" morality in the first place.

Is There Such a Thing as Objective Morality?

For any sort of moral principles to be objective, they would have to be unchanging and apply to all people in all circumstances. As theists often like to point out, one way (or, according to theists, the only way) to have some sort of objective morality would be to have it imposed from an external source such as a god of some sort, in which case morality becomes whatever that god says to do or not do. Unfortunately, even if you believe in a god of some sort (which I don't), using a god as the source of objective morality quickly becomes an exercise in futility because:

- Different people believe in different gods (or different concepts of the same god).

- Nobody can agree upon what, exactly, their god has said to do and not do, even among members of the same religious communities.

- Many of the things various gods have supposedly told their followers to do and not do thousands of years ago seem to have been tailored specifically for the culture in which his followers lived back then (Gee, an "objective" morality that changes over time, go figure…).

- None of these gods are apparently willing to provide any clarification today to clear up the various misinterpretations regarding their moral principles.

Another way to possibly have some sort of objective morality, however, is to claim that there are fundamental laws of nature that somehow dictate what is "good" and "bad" when it comes to how we treat our fellow man. I know a number of atheists who really try to make this argument, presumably so that they can silence the theists who keep claiming that atheists can't be moral since they have no basis for objective morality. I'm not entirely swayed by this, however.

First of all, I'm not at all swayed by the claim that objective morality is even needed in the first place to be moral. Morality is a set of principles that govern how we act toward one another, and one can follow those principles regardless of whether those principles are based on some "objective" or "absolute" standards or laws.

Second of all, I'm not convinced that there are any absolute natural laws or principles that determine (or can be used to determine) whether our actions are objectively "good" or "moral." At most, I think that humans have, on the whole, an innate sense of empathy toward each other that tends to make us feel happy when others are happy and sad when others are sad, and that can certainly form the basis of a general principle of "treat others the way you want to be treated," but that only goes so far. That innate empathy often only extends to members of our immediate family or tribe, and sometimes doesn't even go that far. It is also possible to derive some general moral principles from our long experience with civilization and our experimental discovery of what sorts of laws best help a society to run smoothly. Once again, though, I hesitate to call these in any way "objective" or "absolute" since so many different societies and cultures throughout recorded history have come up with radically different laws.

The closest thing to any sort of "objective" morality I think we could ever really come up with is the simple realization that all humans are equally deserving of the same respect simply be virtue of being human. Different actions and situations may warrant different treatment, but the underlying principle of respect would remain a constant.

"Objective" vs. "Subjective" Morality

Many theists like to attack atheists for not having any basis to determine "right" from "wrong" and "good" from "evil". Often, the attack goes something along the lines of, "If atheists don't believe in God and the Bible and the threat of eternal punishment in Hell, what keeps them from just going around and raping, killing, robbing, etc.?" The underlying assumption being, of course, that atheists can only look to "subjective" morality, if anything, while theists get their "objective" moral standards straight from God. The following essay is my response to hearing this argument for nearly the thousandth time.

Morality — the system or method by which we determine whether actions are "good" or "bad" — can either be "objective" (a.k.a. "absolute") or "subjective" (a.k.a. "relative"). **Objective** or **absolute** morality is morality based on universal principles that everybody agrees on and that do not change over time or from one culture to another, whereas **subjective** or **relative** morality is determined differently by different groups and is subject to change over time and in different places and cultures. Now, theists and atheists alike claim to be able to determine right from wrong, good from bad, but what type of morality can each group actually claim to have? Objective or subjective?

Let's start with atheists. Now *most* atheists get their sense of "right" and "wrong" from the realization that other people are human beings the same as they are, and are therefore deserving of the exact same rights and respect as themselves. "People are people" may sound like a simple tautology, but it's objectively true and it's the core principle that provides atheists with the **objective** morality that lets them condemn slavery, murder, robbery, lying, etc. Now, this isn't to say that all atheists are good people, since we all have free will and can decide whether to be good or bad, but at least atheists have something objective by which they can make value judgments in the first place.

What about theists? Well, they tend to rely more on wholly **subjective** morality to make value judgments for the following reasons:

First, different theists believe in different Gods, each of which is said to have given different moral laws for us to follow. So, right there, theistic morality is wholly subjective based on which God you believe in.

Second, even within a single God belief (Christianity, say), there are tons and tons of different denominations and sects who all interpret the supposed "word of God" in different ways from a purely doctrinal standpoint. So, once again, even within the Christian faith, theistic morality is wholly relative subjective based on which particular sect or denomination you belong to.

Third, even within a single sect or denomination, it's pretty much guaranteed that different preachers or even individual members will have their own specific interpretations as to just what their God wants them to do. Should you shun homosexuals or welcome them? Should you donate money to homeless people or is that just encouraging bad habits? Do women really need to be subject to their husbands' will or not? Is it enough to just accept Jesus into your heart, or do you actually need to do good deeds and repent for your sins? Is it really harder for a rich man to enter the kingdom of heaven than it is for a camel to pass through the eye of a needle, or is that just a metaphor? Does "turn the other cheek" mean you can't own a gun for self-defense? Did God really just promise to "answer prayers" (and sometimes the answer is "no") or did he actually promise to give "whatsoever we ask for in faith"? Is lusting after a woman in your heart really the same as committing adultery, or was Jesus just being metaphorical again? What's the best way to "love thy neighbor as thyself" while still preventing transgender people from using the bathroom they feel most comfortable in? Is it OK to vote for somebody who claims to share your values if he talks about sexually assaulting women, mocks disabled people and lies all the time? What, actually, would Jesus do? And so on and so forth. Thus, theistic morality is wholly subjective based on the individual beliefs of each particular theist.

Finally, for theists that claim to get their morality from Holy Scriptures written thousands of years ago, many of the oldest commandments and moral codes from those books no longer apply today. The explanation for this is usually that those commandments were given for a specific group of people, that the culture and socio-economic conditions back then were different than they are today and/or that some sort of "new covenant" made those old commandments obsolete. It was OK to own slaves back then, but not today. It was commanded that disobedient children should be stoned to death back then, but we don't need to follow that commandment today. Jews were required to keep kosher, but later Christians didn't need to. All of which is to say that theistic morality can actually change over time and is wholly subjective based on the particular people to whom the moral commandments were given.

Now, keep in mind what I said earlier about atheists basing their morality on objective principles. Because these principles are objective, theists are capable of perceiving them as well. In fact, this is what allows, say, Christians to decide which parts of the Bible to follow in the first place and which parts should be ignored or reinterpreted away. The problem is, though, that many theists allow these objective moral principles to be overwhelmed by the teachings of their particular religion to the point where they are willing to discriminate against other people simply because this is what they have been *taught* is correct. Without the teachings of their religion they may never feel it right to, say, kill an infidel, or deny homosexuals the right to marry or treat other people as property. But because they have been indoctrinated to accept the relative morality provided by their religion, they end up chucking objective morality right out the window.

Now this isn't to say that all theists are bad people or incapable of making moral judgments. After all, just because a moral principle is relative doesn't mean it is wrong. But it does mean that their sense of right and wrong is at the whim of their religious indoctrination and this is why a lot of otherwise good people can be convinced to do some very bad things (or, as Nobel prize-winning physicist Steven Weinberg once put it, "With or without [religion] you would have good people doing good things and evil people doing evil things. But for good people to do evil things, that takes religion.") In other words, without a source of objective morals to rely on, theists can only do what they are told is right, regardless of whether it actually *is* right.

Morality and Religion

A lot of theists claim to get their sense of morality directly from their religious beliefs and, as a result, they seem to be unable to comprehend how atheists can possibly have any sense of morality without a belief in God (and specifically the particular God they happen to believe in, of course). Or perhaps they acknowledge that atheists do have a sense of morality, but just desperately want atheists to acknowledge that such a sense of morality could only come from God (and, once again, specifically the particular God they happen to believe in, of course), which would somehow magically get atheists to finally declare that God must exist after all.

Whatever.

The point is, however, that these theists are convinced that morality and religion are inextricably linked somehow. But is it? Do theists really get their morality from their religion and religious beliefs? The following are my thoughts on the matter, completely unsupported by any scientific research whatsoever, but hopefully enlightening nonetheless…

First of all, we need to define what we mean by "morality" in the first place. For the sake of this discussion, I am going to define morality broadly as "a method of determining how to act in various situations." Words like "good" and "bad" and "right" and "wrong" get bandied about when discussing morality, but people don't agree on what those terms mean and frequently attempt to define them in a way that assumes the point they are arguing (for example, defining "good" as "what God wants us to do" presupposes that God exists in a circular sort of way). So, for now, let's just leave it as "a method of determining how to act," shall we?

Now, before religions got involved in things, I think it's pretty clear that the way people determined how to act (especially toward other people) was determined by two primary factors:

1. The innate sense of empathy that most humans are born with that lets us feel pleasure when seeing other people enjoying themselves and feel discomfort when seeing other people in pain or distress.

2. A realization, partially inborn and partially learned from experience, of what sorts of behaviors let us live together with our fellow human beings as the cooperative and social animals that we are.

These two factors let most cultures throughout the world figure out that killing other people is bad, that it's important to treat each other the way we want to be treated, that we shouldn't lie, steal, cheat, etc.

So, where do religions come into this? Well, many religions take these basic concepts and codify them as "official laws from God," which is all well and good in principle. Unfortunately, religions tend to then go ahead and add a whole bunch of unnatural laws to their moral code such as the importance of worshiping a particular god, prohibition against various sexual practices, dietary restrictions, dress codes, etc., etc., etc. And people accept these additions as valid primarily because, well, the ones about not killing or lying or stealing seem so reasonable, don't they? And if this god you're talking about gave us those laws, well, it must know what it's talking about, right?

Another problem with religious-based morals is that each individual religion can claim to have special knowledge from their own particular "objective" source (a.k.a. their deity), leading to extreme amounts of dogmatism. Each religion "knows" that their moral code is divinely inspired and correct, which means that everybody else is a sinner (despite the fact that they may have their very own moral code that they also "know" is divinely inspired and correct). Unfortunately, no matter how many times members of one particula religion claim to have a source of "objective" or "absolute" morality, the fact that every religion has its own set means that these morals are the very definition of "subjective" in the first place.

A third problem with religious-based morals is that, while much of the moral code of a particular religion may be perfectly in line with our natural empathetic instincts, it opens the door for people in power to claim that their particular god has commanded them to do some truly horrific acts, including the wholesale slaughter of other people, killing of non-believers, female genital mutilation, discrimination against those who do not share their beliefs, denial of scientific facts when action is required to help other people, etc. Or, to quote Steven Weinberg once again, "With or without [religion] you would have good people doing good things and evil people doing evil things. But for good people to do evil things, that takes religion."

Do We Even Need a Moral Framework?

Theists often ask questions about atheism and morality in an attempt to either attack atheists as somehow being incapable of having morals or in an attempt to prove that God must exist if atheists claim to have morals. In either case, the assumption/assertion is always that so-called "objective" or "absolute" morals can only possibly come from God (and, of course, the specific God the particular theists believes in and not any of the other thousands of gods worshiped by other theists throughout history), and therefore atheists must either acknowledge that they don't have "objective" or "absolute" morals (which, apparently, is the only type of acceptable morals) or else acknowledge that they secretly do believe in God after all.

In my previous essays on the subject of morality, I have discussed the whole question of whether "objective" or "absolute" morality is even possible in the first place and, if so, who actually has a better claim to it. This time, however, I want to address one particular flavor of this perennial question about where atheists get their morality or whether atheists can even have morals in the first place, and that is as follows:

"Where do atheists get their moral framework?"

Now, at first glance, this might simply be a rephrasing of "where do atheists get their morals" or "how can atheists be moral," but I think it actually is a bit more insidious than that. Because, you see, despite the fact that I have talked numerous times about how atheists (just like theists) get our basic morality from our innate sense of empathy that allows us to recognize other people as fellow human beings, I have always acknowledged that this is really just a *baseline* or a *foundation* for morality and not any type of structured set of moral codes or laws. Which then leaves atheists open to the accusation that we either do not have a structured set of moral codes or laws (a "framework") or else we can only get that framework from God the way theists do.

After giving this some thought, however, I realize that it's actually not necessary to explain *how* atheists come up with a detailed moral framework since the whole notion that we actually *need* such a framework in the first place is purely the invention of theists who think they *have* such a framework. It's basically a variation of a common theme we see in many questions from theists toward atheists:

> *"Since theists get their purpose in life from God, where do atheists get their purpose in life?"*

> *"Since theists explain the origin of the universe by saying 'God did it,' how do atheists explain where the universe came from?"*

> *"Since theists cope with death by accepting that God provides them with an afterlife, how can atheists possibly cope with death?"*

> *"Since theists get their moral framework 'from God' (or more properly, from their particular religion's interpretation of their particular set of scriptures), where do atheists get their moral framework from?"*

The one thing all these questions have in common is an assumption on the part of the theist that, just because *they* use their religion and belief in God as a crutch to get through life, everybody else must be unable to get through life without also having a crutch of some sort. Except, of course, this assumption is unfounded and is typically the result of being indoctrinated from an early age that life is meaningless and empty and chaotic (and nasty and brutish and short) if you don't have God in your life (speaking from personal experience here, mind you).

But who says that we actually *need* to find a purpose in life? Many people either define their own purpose or else just go on living their lives as they see fit without ever considering any sort of deeper meaning or purpose to what they are doing. Just because you can't live your life without somebody giving you a purpose doesn't mean that we can't.

And who says that we actually *need* to explain where the universe came from? Many people live their entire lives perfectly satisfied without knowing the answers to the "big questions" that theists think are so important. Just because *you* can't be satisfied without having somebody provide you with an answer (whether actually true or not) doesn't mean that *we* can't be.

And who says that we actually *need* to "cope" with death? Death is a part of life. Everything that has ever been born eventually dies (well, except perhaps for a few species of jellyfish). We don't have to "cope" with death — we just *accept* it as part of reality and live our lives. Just because *you* can't accept reality and therefore must make up fairy stories to provide you with a way of avoiding thinking about it doesn't mean that *we* have any problem accepting reality.

And, finally, who says that we actually *need* any sort of formalized "moral framework" in order to live our lives as part of civilized society? As I mentioned earlier, most people are born with a natural sense of empathy that lets us recognize other people as fellow human beings and makes us feel bad when we see other people suffering, and as a result we tend to not actually want to make other people suffer. We don't spend our lives pondering what we would do in hypothetical situations — we just live our lives, trying hard not to hurt anybody, trying to help other people when we can, and obeying the laws of the land in which we live. Just because *you* can't live your lives without constantly referring to ancient books written thousands of years ago by people who thought it was OK to own slaves, kill homosexuals and disobedient children, etc., doesn't mean that *we* are unable to do so.

Chapter 11. The Demands of Justice, the Mercy of God and the Sacrifice of Jesus

Back when I was a practicing Christian, one of the things I had the hardest time understanding was how a loving God could condemn any of his children to eternal torment. The standard explanations I got usually went along the lines that God doesn't actually *condemn* anybody to Hell; instead, people *choose* to go there themselves by not accepting and following God's word. And then there would be some discussion about the importance of free will and how God can't force anybody to be good.

Underlying this explanation, however, are the core concepts of **Divine Justice** and **Divine Mercy**. Divine Justice, it is said, is an absolute principle that demands that a price is paid for every sin. That's just the way it is. If you sin, you need to be punished for it. However, because God loves us all so very, very much, He decided to come up with a way to let us off the hook. Since the demands of Divine Justice are so incredibly powerful, God figured out that the only way to get around those demands was to have an all-powerful being sacrifice Himself for everybody else's sake. To, in effect, take responsibility for the sins of the entire world, to take the blame, and therefore pay the price Himself. And that is why He decided to send His only begotten Son (or send Himself, depending on what version of Christianity you adhere to) to suffer and die on the cross for us. And why would He do this? Why, because He is a loving God who believes in being merciful. After all, wouldn't you spare your children pain and suffering if you had the power to do so?

Of course, this Divine Mercy has a catch to it. God isn't just going to be merciful to every Tom, Dick or Harry who wants to avoid being tormented for all eternity. No, if God is going to go to all this trouble to sacrifice His Son (or Himself, if you prefer), then the least we can do is acknowledge that sacrifice and do a few small things like be baptized, pray to Him, try to keep His commandments, ask for forgiveness each and every time we make a mistake, maybe donate to His church (whichever one that actually is), etc. No big deal, right? And anybody who isn't willing to put in that teeny bit of effort in order to be saved, well, they deserve to burn in hell for all eternity for being such ungrateful little pricks, right?

OK, so obviously I'm embellishing the explanation a bit. What is typically said is simply along the lines of the following:

"Justice demands that our sins are punished, and God's mercy allows us to escape that punishment if we choose to accept it."

But the implications are all there. And here's where it all breaks down to me:

First of all, why does Divine Justice demand that all sins are punished? And who decided that all sins are equally punishable with eternal torment? If God created the universe and is truly omnipotent, then He made the rules in the first place and can change them as He sees fit, right? If cheating on a test warrants the same punishment as committing genocide and the punishment for both is *eternal freaking torment*, where's the justice in that ("Divine" or otherwise)? Instead of providing a "loophole," why wouldn't a merciful God just not set up a system of ridiculously draconian and over-the-top "justice" in the first place? I'm not even talking about getting rid of punishment altogether, mind you [Christian folk really do seem to love the idea of the guilty getting their just deserts, don't they?], but simply making the punishment fit the crime and acknowledging that **no** crime is worthy of *eternal freaking torment*!

Second of all, even if you want to argue that the draconian justice system is OK since God has provided an easy way to avoid that justice, this ignores the fact that the vast, vast majority of humanity will never actually be able to take part of that mercy. Even if you could figure out which of all the many different Christian denominations is the "right" one to follow, for most of human history Christianity either didn't exist or was a small minority belief. Even today, there are billions of people who are born, live their entire lives, and die without ever having the chance to hear about God's merciful offer[12]. And even if they do hear the offer, no evidence whatsoever is ever provided to convince people to abandon their beliefs and switch over to the correct religion (whatever one that happens to be).

So, the bottom line is that God supposedly set up a system whereby any sin is punishable by eternal torment, and then decided "in His mercy" to create a loophole that the majority of His children would either never have a chance to accept or would have no good reason to accept, effectively condemning the vast majority of humanity to suffer in agony for all time and eternity through no fault of their own.

Gee, what a guy!

---

[12] I should note, by the way, that the Church of Jesus Christ of Latter-day Saints (a.k.a. "The Mormon Church") has come up with a way to deal with this problem. Or at least to *attempt* to deal with it. True, not everybody will have a chance to hear the Gospel during their lifetime, but anybody who didn't will have another chance in the next life. And, since baptism is an absolute requirement for salvation, Mormons therefore perform many thousands of "proxy" baptisms on behalf of all those who might decide to accept the gospel in the next life. Unfortunately for this proposed solution, though, (a) I don't think they'll ever get all the billions of people who lived and died without hearing the Gospel and (b) that still leaves all those who heard the gospel in this life and didn't choose to accept it for whatever reason. Mormons further get around the idea of "eternal torment" by claiming that those who reject the gospel even after hearing it won't actually be sent to hell but will instead get to live in the "Terrestrial Kingdom" of heaven, which is basically just like earth but without all the disease and natural disasters. So, no eternal glory with God, but not a bad place to be. For *all time and freaking eternity!*

On a related note, Christians often point to Jesus's sacrifice on the cross as something that sets Christianity apart from all other world religions. In particular, God decided to come to Earth in a mortal form and allow himself to be crucified to pay the price for the sins of all people, thereby giving those who believe in him the ability to spend eternity in heaven with him instead of spending eternity being tortured in hell. And this, they claim, just shows how much God loves us since there is nothing more virtuous than somebody giving up his own life to save that of others, right?

Except, of course, if Jesus Christ is actually God, then he couldn't really "give up his life" in the first place, could he? And even if you claim that his mortal body did, in fact, die, he knew that he was going to come back to life three days later any way, right? So was it *really* that much of a sacrifice, or more of a minor inconvenience?

And why was such a "sacrifice" even required in the first place for people to go to heaven instead of being tortured eternally in hell? Many Christians claim that humans are "born sinners" (either because of their inherent nature or due to Adam and Eve's "original sin" depending on which Christians you ask) and therefore simply cannot enter into the Kingdom of God unless there is some way to rid themselves of their sin, but wouldn't God have been the one to set up such a system in the first place? Who decreed that all of humanity must bear the price of Adam and Eve's original sin or would otherwise be born sinners? And who decreed that anybody who is not "cleansed of sin" must be tortured forever in hell? If God set up a system whereby the default state of humanity was to be tortured forever as a result of simply being born, is it really such a "virtuous" thing that he also provided a loophole through which a very small percentage of humanity could avoid that fate he himself decreed?

In order to better understand why Jesus's sacrifice on the cross wasn't any sort of virtuous act deserving praise and worship, allow me offer the following analogy:

> King Omnithrax is the absolute monarch of the country Erehwon, although he never leaves his castle and some people in the kingdom doubt whether he even really exists. His castle is immense and, although nobody has ever actually seen the inside of it and returned, it is said that there are millions of luxurious rooms and a constant supply of good food (unlike conditions in the rest of the country, where life is hard and food is scarce).
>
> Now King Omnithrax thinks that it's really, really important that all of his subjects follow all of his many, many laws. And so, he sets up a system of reward and punishment to encourage this. At the age of 50, every single subject will be judged. If the subject has led a spotless life without ever violating any of the laws, then they are allowed to move into one of the many rooms in the castle and spend the rest of their lives in a state of luxury and bliss. If, however, the subject has violated any laws whatsoever — even minor ones like spitting in public or driving one mile over the speed limit, they will instead be tortured to death.
>
> Now, you might think it is awfully harsh of King Omnithrax to punish even minor infractions with death by torture, but you need to understand that he loves his subjects so much that he created a special loophole to allow even those who break the law to avoid torture and come and live with him instead. You see, one day (long after tens of thousands of his subjects had already reached the age of 50 and been tortured to death), he decided to dress up as one of his subjects and sneak into town, upon which he allowed himself to be put in jail overnight and be forced to eat "peasant" food. Oh, what a sacrifice it was! But the important thing was that since he, the king, had "paid the price" for a crime he didn't actually commit, he could now use his own sacrifice as a legal justification for forgiving other people for their crimes

that they actually did *commit. Because, of course, there was simply no other way for him to forgive people of their crimes (despite the fact that he was an absolute monarch who made all the laws and determined the penalties for all crimes in the first place).*

Of course, King Omnithrax didn't actually tell *everybody about what he had done. No, he just told a few people who happened to be near the jail when he exited and changed back into his kingly garb and left it to them to spread the word, making it very clear to them that he would only forgive the crimes of those who actually believed he existed, believed that he had performed such a great sacrifice for them and performed a bunch of very specific ritualistic acts to show their belief and their sincerity.*

And so, over time, a bunch of people heard the story of what King Omnithrax had done and what he said was required for people to have their crimes forgiven. Not everybody heard the story, of course. And many of those who heard the story thought it was rather silly and didn't believe it (especially those who didn't even think the King was real to begin with). And, of course, the story itself changed over time as different people retold it until nobody was really sure exactly what had happened and what they were supposed to actually do. But, it all worked out well in the end as a very small percentage of King Omnithrax's subjects did indeed believe and figure out what they needed to do in order to be saved, and they did go live happily ever after in the King's castle after turning 50.

Oh — and everybody else got tortured to death upon turning 50. But, hey — that's was entirely on them since it was their fault for not believing in the king and what he had done and for not doing everything the king said to do, right?

Now, tell me. Was King Omnithrax a "virtuous" and loving ruler who performed a great sacrifice in order to give his beloved subjects a way to come and live with him and enjoy a life of luxury? Or was he instead a monstrous despot who set up a system whereby the vast majority of his subjects would end up being tortured to death despite also providing a loophole that would enable a select few to avoid that fate?

Chapter 12.   Christianity's "Adam and Eve" Problem

The story of Adam and Eve in the Garden of Eden appears in the Hebrew Tanakh (a.k.a. the "Jewish Bible" or "The Old Testament") and, as such, was written specifically for the Jewish people living at the time the story was written. And it's important to realize that Jews at the time (and, for the most part, today) did not have any concept of a heaven or a hell or any sort of afterlife whatsoever, as evidenced by this passage in Ecclesiastes 9: 5-6:

> For the living know that they shall die: but the dead know not any thing, neither have they any more a reward; for the memory of them is forgotten.

> Also their love, and their hatred, and their envy, is now perished; neither have they any more a portion for ever in any thing that is done under the sun.

If anything, the story was written to explain why daily life as a member of God's "chosen people" was often so hard — "We had a shot at paradise and screwed it up, so now we have to toil away every day just to survive." And that really was it. No hope of redemption or someday being reunited with God in His kingdom, just an acknowledgement that life is hard and we need to worship God regardless of that fact because He's the one who created us.

When Christianity came on the scene many hundreds of years later, however, it purposely used the Hebrew scriptures as a foundation upon which to base its own validity. Which is why so many of the stories of Jesus's birth and life and death contain so many oddly specific details since the anonymous authors of the Gospels (written many years after the events depicted, of course) tried very hard to link Jesus to anything that could even remotely be considered a prophecy in the Tanakh. With varying degrees of success, of course (such as when they relied a mistranslation in the Greek Septuagint to claim that Jesus was born of a "virgin" instead of simply a "young woman" as in the original Hebrew version).

As part of this adoption of the Hebrew Tanakh, Christianity also adopted the story of Adam and Eve in the Garden of Eden. Except, unlike the Jews who had no concept of heaven or hell or any sort of an afterlife, the Christian doctrine was quite clear that (a) there was indeed a heaven, (b) only those who hear the words of Jesus and follow them will be welcome in heaven, and (c) everybody else would be condemned to an eternity in hell. At which point, of course, the story of Adam and Eve became more than just an explanation for why life is hard and turned into a reason for why Jesus's life and death were necessary. And, as part of this, it also served as the explanation for exactly why anybody who didn't follow Jesus was doomed to an eternity of suffering. It also provided Christianity (which, unlike Judaism, has always been a proselytizing religion) with both a carrot and a stick to convince others to join — believe and go to heaven, disbelieve and go to hell!

Sadly for Christianity, the story of Adam and Eve in the Garden of Eden really isn't a good fit for the additional doctrine that Christianity chose to layer on top of Judaism and it poses some real problems for those actually willing to consider the ramifications of doing so. And this is true whether a Christian wants to consider the story to be literally true or merely a metaphor.

Let's start with the idea that the story is, in fact, literally true. God created Adam and Eve, placed them in a beautiful garden, told them not to eat the fruit of one particular tree, and then punished them (and their descendants as well as the entire natural world) when they disobeyed him. And that's why we are all born as cursed sinners and why we need the saving grace and sacrifice of Jesus in order to be cleansed and be worthy to return to God's presence after we die. OK, so what are the problematic ramifications of all this? Why, I'm so glad you asked:

First of all, the one tree whose fruit Adam and Eve were specifically forbidden to partake of was actually called "**The Tree of Knowledge of Good and Evil**." Which, of course, means that Adam and Eve couldn't have known the difference between good and evil until after they had eaten the fruit of that tree. Yes, they disobeyed God, but **they had no way of knowing that doing so was a bad thing**. And God, of course, knew this, which means the entire thing was a setup from the beginning (who do you think allowed the serpent to enter the garden and tempt them?). Which means that God is a total bastard.

Second of all, just because Adam and Eve supposedly "sinned" by eating the forbidden fruit, why would God need to curse all of their descendants? Or, to put it in catholic terms, why would that cause every one of their descendants to be born with "original sin"? What sort of total bastard punishes somebody for what their great-great-great-times-a-hundred-grandparents did?

Third of all, while Christian apologists often point to "free will" as an explanation for why there is so much suffering in the world, that only serves as an explanation for suffering caused by man's inhumanity to man (often in the name of religion, but I digress). When it comes to all the rest of the suffering in the natural world (natural disasters, genetic diseases, parasitical infections, viruses, flesh eating bacteria, birth defects, etc.) the explanation is usually either that all those things are the work of Satan (which then raises the question of why a loving and omnipotent God would actually allow Satan to cause all that suffering) or else that the sin of Adam and Eve somehow caused the entire natural world to enter into a fallen state (as if that somehow absolved God of any of the fault). Except, of course, that God would necessarily have been the one to set up the whole system in the first place, wouldn't He? If He is truly omnipotent, He certainly could have set things up differently so that, say, only humanity needed to suffer in life without giving Tasmanian

Devils facial tumors. Unless, of course, he's just a total bastard who likes seeing cute little animals needless suffer.

The list could go on and on, of course, but the bottom line is that if the story of Adam and Eve in the Garden of Eden is literally true then it just proves that the god of Christianity is a complete and utter bastard who is petty, vindictive and cruel.

But what if it's not actually meant to be taken literally? What if, as many Christians claim, it's meant to simply be a metaphor to explain that humans are naturally sinful and thus in need of Jesus's saving grace? The "original sin" in this case is simply the fact of being born human since humans by their very nature are too unclean to enter into the presence of a perfect being such as God without some help. Sounds perfectly reasonable, right? Well, except for the fact that:

On the one hand, if humans are naturally imperfect, unclean and sinful, whose fault is that? Even if the story of Adam and Eve in the Garden of Eden isn't literally true, it still means that God is responsible for creating us the way we are, sinful nature and all. An omnipotent God certainly could have created us to be naturally without any desire to do evil whatsoever, but instead he chose to make us this way. What sort of total bastard creates something imperfect on purpose and then punished that creation for being imperfect?

On the other hand, if all humans are born too unclean to enter the kingdom of heaven and avoid an eternity in hell unless we accept the saving grace of Jesus, why would a supposedly omnipotent and loving God make it so hard for the vast, vast majority of His children to know about this "loophole"? Could there possibly have been any less efficient way of spreading the word than to give it to a bunch of mostly illiterate desert nomads who would take hundreds of years to spread it just to the surrounding regions and thousands of years to the rest of the world? And couldn't He take some precautions to make sure His word wouldn't get corrupted over time or that it would be clear enough that different groups wouldn't interpret it in different ways? And couldn't He make sure that no other competing religions would arise and convince people that they were the ones that were the real One True Faith™? What sort of total bastard makes eternal life and the avoidance of eternal punishment contingent on hearing and understanding and believing one particular message and then doesn't care whether that message is able to be clearly transmitted to everybody who needs to hear it?

So, where does all this get us? Well, if the story of Adam and Eve in the Garden of Eden is literally true, then God is a complete and utter bastard for punishing all of us (and perhaps the entire natural world) for a sin that our distant ancestors couldn't have possibly have even realized was a sin when they committed it. And if the story of Adam and Eve in the Garden of Eden is just a metaphor, then God is a complete and utter bastard for creating us as impure, sinful creatures and then condemning the majority of us to an eternity of torment simply for having been born.

Either way, the story of Adam and Eve in the Garden of Eden just proves that the Christian god is a complete and utter bastard.

Pardon my French.

Chapter 13.   Is America a Christian Nation?

Time and again, when ostensibly devout Christians here in America want to exercise their right to discriminate against those who do not share their beliefs, they trot out the well-worn nostrum that "America is a Christian nation" or "America was founded on Judeo-Christian values" as a justification. This "foundation on Judeo-Christian values" bit is so important, in fact, that some people even think its appropriate to put large stone monuments commemorating the Ten Commandments in courthouses.

But was America or its laws actually founded on Judeo-Christian values (to the exclusion, presumably, of all other values)?

Well, to start with, we have the First Amendment to the United States Constitution, which states in part:

> *Congress shall make no law respecting an establishment of religion…*

So, given the fact that the founders certainly *could* have specifically stated that America was a Christian nation founded on Judeo-Christian values and instead chose to state that would be no official state religion, it certainly *seems* as though the founders at least didn't think that their new country was a Christian nation founded on Judeo-Christian values. But maybe that was just an oversight on their part.

Well, what about Article Six of the very same Constitution, which states in part:

> *[N]o religious Test shall ever be required as a Qualification to any Office or public Trust under the United States.*

Again, the founders *could* have stated that only good, God-fearing Christians would be eligible to serve in public office, but instead chose to say that it essentially didn't matter what religion (if any) somebody belonged to. Still, maybe they just *assumed* that all Americans would be Christians and this was to prevent bickering between, say, Catholics and Protestants. Hey — it's possible, right?

And then, of course, we have the famous "Separation of Church and State" as described by Thomas Jefferson:

> *I contemplate with sovereign reverence that act of the whole American people which declared that their legislature should "make no law respecting an establishment of religion, or prohibiting the free exercise thereof," thus building a wall of separation between Church & State.*

But surely Thomas Jefferson was an outlier, right? One wacky "deist" in a sea of devout Christians, obviously. Surely the rest of the founders and early Americans were confident that America was, first and foremost, a Christian nation and were not afraid to announce this fact openly, right? Well, not according to the Treaty of Tripoli, which was submitted to the Senate by President John Adams, received **unanimous** ratification from the U.S. Senate on June 7, 1797, and states in part:

> *As the Government of the United States of America is not, in any sense, founded on the Christian religion; as it has in itself no character of enmity against the laws, religion, or tranquility, of Mussulmen [Muslims]; and as the said States never entered into any war or act of hostility against any Mahometan nation, it is declared by the parties that no pretext arising from religious opinions shall ever produce an interruption of the harmony existing between the two countries.*

But, hey — maybe they were just lying for the sake of getting the treaty done. Not that lying is exactly a "Christian" value, mind you, but that's politics for you.

OK, so depending on your point of view, it's either blindingly obvious that the founders of this great country did not think that America was founded on Judeo-Christian values or else it's blindingly obvious that none of the facts provided above have anything whatsoever to do with the issue and can be safely ignored ("Nothing to see here, folks, move along"). Fine. For those in the latter camp, however, how about we explore exactly what these supposed "Judeo-Christian values" actually *are* and see if they *do*, in fact, form the foundation of our laws.

First up, of course, is the **Ten Commandments**, which is seen by many American Christians to be the foundation of U.S. law, to the extent that some would erect statues of the 10 Commandments right in the lobby of courthouses, as mentioned earlier. There are various versions, but here's the most common list:

1. Thou shalt have no other gods before me

Hmmmm… I don't see that enshrined anywhere in the Constitution or other laws of the United States. In fact, as mentioned above, the First Amendment of the Constitution specifically says that "Congress shall make no law respecting an establishment of religion, or prohibiting the free exercise thereof." You'd think that if America were indeed founded on Judeo-Christian values the first and arguably most important commandment would be called out somewhere, right? Interesting…

2. Thou shalt not make unto thee any graven image

Hmmmm… Again, I don't see anything about this mentioned anywhere in the Constitution or other laws of the United States. And it's kinda ironic that somebody would fight to erect a large graven image of the 10 Commandments in front of a court of law, doncha think?

3. Thou shalt not take the name of the Lord thy God in vain

Nope, still not seeing it. One could argue, by the way, that putting "In God We Trust" on our money is a direct violation of this commandment. There's a reason why observant Jews write "G-D" instead of "God". Ah, well... moving on!

4. Remember the sabbath day, to keep it holy

Ah, yes — this must be why we have all those laws prohibiting football games and NASCAR races on Sundays. Oh wait, never mind. As an aside, did anybody else find it hilarious when, after 9/11, everybody started singing "God Bless America" at sporting events held on Sundays? Just me, huh? OK, fine.

5. Honour thy father and thy mother

You know, the Old Testament was really explicit about this one. In fact, Deuteronomy 21:18-21 specifically states that if you have a disobedient child, you need to take them outside and have them *stoned to death*. Gotta love those old time family values! Regardless, I'm not aware of anything in the Constitution or other laws of the land dealing with this.

6. Thou shalt not kill

Bingo! We have a winner! This one is *definitely* in the Constitution. Isn't it? OK, so it actually isn't. We *do* have the nifty Second Amendment right to bear arms, though, so I guess it's OK to kill in *some* circumstances. But, what the heck — let's give this one to them, since there are plenty of English common law statutes dating back hundreds of years that prohibit murder.

7. Thou shalt not commit adultery

Um, yeah. Sorry, no laws against adultery. Which is good, I suppose, since most of the politicians would be in jail. Remember back in 2012 and the only Republican running for president that hadn't had more than one wife was the Mormon? Good times, good times.

8. Thou shalt not steal

Again, not in the Constitution, but plenty of examples from English common law. So we'll give it to the Christians. That's what, 2 out of 8 so far? Hmmmm… In other news, it's a darn good thing that "steal" doesn't include manipulating the tax code to avoid paying ones fair share of taxes to contribute to the common good, right? I mean, am I right, or am I right?

9. Thou shalt not bear false witness against thy neighbor

Not really sure about this one, to be honest. Nothing in the Constitution (again), but plenty of laws regarding perjury in a court of law. That probably counts, so that makes 3 of 9 so far. w00t!

10. Thou shalt not covet (thy neighbor's house, wife, servants, animals, or anything else)

OK, I'm going to go out on a limb here and call this commandment positively un-American on its face. I mean coveting your neighbor's, well, *everything*, is what capitalism is all about and is what makes this country so great in the first place, capisce? Well, maybe not *quite*, but there still ain't any laws against it, and that's a fact!

OK, so the final tally from the Ten Commandments is a pretty poor showing of only 3 out of 10. Maybe. Not looking so good for this myth so far, but let's see what a selection of values described in the **New** Testament can tell us:

"Thou shalt love the Lord thy God with all thy heart, and with all thy soul, and with all thy mind (Matthew 22:37)."

Nope, just a restatement of the first of the 10 Commandments. Nothing to do with the U.S. And remember, according to the Biblical account, Jesus said this was the most important commandment of all, so it seems odd not to have it actually enshrined anywhere in our laws.

"Thou shalt love thy neighbor as thyself (Matthew 22:39)."

[Nice enough sentiment (and in no way original to Christ's teachings), but not really enshrined anywhere or officially part of U.S. values.

"Religion that God our Father accepts as pure and faultless is this: to look after orphans and widows in their distress and to keep oneself from being polluted by the world (James 1:27)."

It's interesting how so many conservative Christians think we need laws to prevent gay marriage and abortions due to "Bible principles" and yet rail against government programs that "force people" (via taxes) to care for the poor, the widowed, the orphans, etc. Suddenly, it's a bad thing for the government to "force" anybody to follow Biblical principles (when it's a principle they don't actually want to follow themselves, of course). I'm just saying…

"Ye have heard that it hath been said, An eye for an eye, and a tooth for a tooth: But I say unto you, That ye resist not evil: but whosoever shall smite thee on thy right cheek, turn to him the other also. And if any man will sue thee at the law, and take away thy coat, let him have thy cloak also (Matthew 5:38-40)."

Well, seeing as how the United States spends more on its military than, what, the next top ten countries combined, I'm going to give this one a big fat "NOPE!" There's also that pesky "right to bear arms" enshrined in the Second Amendment to the Constitution to consider. And as for giving people more than what they ask for if they sue you, well, that alone would put more than half the lawyers in this country out of business, wouldn't it?

"Judge not, that ye be not judged (Matthew 7:1)."

Well, there goes our entire legal system down the drain...

And so on and so forth. Yes, one could try to abstract the "Judeo-Christian values" into some sort of core beliefs like "treat individuals with respect" or something, but that's just a modern gloss on what the scriptures that form the basis of Judeo-Christian values actually state.

And please, don't even get me started on all the other Biblical laws that most modern-day Christians wholly write off as not applicable. I mean, it's vitally important that gay people not be allowed to marry since the Bible says that homosexuality is wrong, but divorce? Eating shrimp? Owning slaves (OK, sorry, that one actually *was* in the Constitution to start with until the 14th Amendment came along...)

Chapter 14.   Trying to Make Sense of Noah's Ark

I don't normally care too much about Young Earth Creationists and other folks who think that every single word and account in the Bible is literally true, since they are in no way in the mainstream among Christians and their assertions are just so easy to debunk. But I have to admit that seeing repeated claims that the story of Noah's Ark is actually "scientifically plausible" always tickles my funny bone, especially when the claim tries to explain how Noah could have really brought two (and sometimes seven) of every single type of animal on earth with him. The following essay was my response to one such claim.

At the time the story of Noah's Ark was first written thousands of years ago, it actually made some sort of sense to talk about building a boat large enough to carry representative samples of each of the various kinds of animal on earth. After all, the people who wrote the story didn't actually *know* about the existence of most of the different species existing on earth. Sure, they knew about camels, horses, goats, cows, sheep, wolves, cats, bears, lions, elephants, etc., but they had no idea whatsoever about, say, kangaroos and koalas, sloths, penguins, opossums, and all the rest of the animals that lived beyond their small universe of experience. So, if you're only talking about hundreds of different species instead of thousands (or millions), then it makes perfect sense to think about somebody building an ark to hold them all.

OK, so maybe not *perfect* sense, since you'd still have to deal with feeding them all, disposing of all their waste, and constructing such a monstrous and unseaworthy vessel in the first place using bronze age technology, but you get the point. Those are all minor issue compared to the big one of fitting millions of animals.

That was then, though. Nowadays, we are fully aware of the vast number of different animals that exist today across the globe and not even the most die-hard, blinded by faith, Young Earth Creationist would ever consider denying the existence of these animals. Nobody goes around claiming that kangaroos are a hoax perpetuated by scientists the way that they might claim that evolution is a hoax. After all, we can all go to zoos and actually *see* many of the animals that were completely unknown to the authors of the Noah story. So, given the fact that there truly are just way too many different species of animals that could ever possibly fit onto a single ark, even the most die-hard, blinded by faith, Young Earth Creationists have to admit that it's just a made-up story, right?

Yeah, right. And Flat-Earthers are all going to finally admit the Earth is round because NASA has provided proof that it has satellites and space stations orbiting the planet. Not gonna happen, sorry.

So, how *do* Biblical literalists still make sense of the story of Noah's Ark given what we now know about the animal kingdom? Well, first of all, they claim that there were certain types of animals that Noah didn't need to bring on board. Sea creatures, for example, could all survive in the water and many species of insects could have probably survived by hanging out on mats of floating vegetation or something similar. Forget the fact that the sudden influx of fresh water and the co-mingling of fresh and salt water would have killed off many marine creatures that have evolved to only live in fresh or salt-water environments. It all sort of makes sense, right?

Second of all, Noah only brought *juvenile* members of each species onto the ark. Little baby animals (even little baby dinosaurs) take up a lot less room and don't eat nearly as much as full-grown adult animals, right? I mean, ignore the fact that this isn't actually mentioned in the Biblical account anywhere, since it *could* have happened, right? Even if it *did* happen that way, though, we're still talking about way too many animals to ever fit into an ark. Which brings us to…

Third, and most important of all, instead of bringing two (or, in some cases, seven) of each **species** of animal onto the ark, Noah brought two (or, in some cases, seven) of each "**kind**" of animal. Now, "kind is not a scientific term, but Young Earth Creationists use a sort of "common sense" approach to determining what is and is not a "kind." For example, instead of bringing representative samples of dogs, coyotes, jackals, dingos, hyenas, etc., on the ark, Noah would have just brought a pair of some "dog-like" creature (perhaps similar to a wolf). Similarly, instead of bringing lions, tigers, jaguars, ocelots, lynxes, etc., Noah just brought a pair of "cats."

So, yeah — perfectly sensible, right?

Except... no. The problem with this explanation is that it requires the speciation of thousands and thousands of different "kinds" to occur over the last 4000 years at a speed which would make an evolutionary biologist blush in embarrassment and without anybody actually noticing it happening (Young earth Creationists love to attack things like evolution by claiming it has never been observed, but then they are perfectly willing to accept this).

Just to out this into perspective, after the ark landed at Mt. Ararat, the descendants of this breeding pair of "felines" would have had to rapidly speciate to produce all the different types of cats we see today. Yes, one breeding pair of "cat" was responsible for all the Lions, Tigers, Jaguars, Panthers, Leopards, Ocelots, Lynxes (Canadian, Iberian and Eurasian), House Cats (all the different breeds), Snow Leopards, African Golden Cats, Asian Golden Cats, Bobcats, Caracals, Chinese Desert Cats, Clouded Leopards, Fishing Cats, Servals, African Wild Cats, Andean Mountain Cats, Black-footed Cats, Bornean Bay Cats, European Wild Cats, Flat-headed Cats, Geoffroy's Cats, Iriomote Cats, Jaguarundi, Jungle Cats, Kodkods, Leopard Cats (different from leopards, mind you), Marbled Cats, Margays, Oncillas, Pallas Cats, Pampas Cat, Pumas (a.k.a Mountain Lions or Cougars), Rusty Spotted Cats and Sand

Cats. And all this happened in the last few thousand years or so without anybody seeing it happen.

And that's just cats, mind you. Repeat the same process with horses (zebras, asses, etc.), dogs (wolves, foxes, coyotes, etc.) and every other "kind" of creature for which we now have many different existing species. All of this happening far more rapidly than has ever been observed in nature, and all without a single person in history ever noticing all these new species miraculously appearing overnight ("Hey — that jaguar just gave birth to an ocelot!").

Oh, and since dinosaurs must have lived at the same time as humans, Noah also had to bring one representative pair of "dinosaurs" on the ark as well, but they were very small. And they died off right after the ark landed. Or else they lived long enough for their offspring to cover the earth with their fossils and then suddenly died off, again without anybody actually seeing it happen even though it would have been happening right in front of us during all of recorded history.

And, of course, not only would this rapid speciation have to occur without anybody ever taking note of it, but you would also need to explain how all the animals managed to travel to all the distant parts of the word where they eventually ended up. How did the Kangaroos and Koalas make it to Australia? How did the Sloths make it to South America? How did the penguins make it to Antarctica?

The only answer to all of these questions that Biblical literalists can provide is, of course, "God did it." How could Noah build an ark big enough to carry all the necessary animals with only Bronze Age technology? God showed him how to do it. How could such a monstrosity be seaworthy? God performed a miracle and kept it afloat. How could all the different "kinds" of animals rapidly speciate and distribute themselves globally? God made it happen. Etc., etc., etc. If you want to believe this, go for it. God is a god of miracles, after all, and with God nothing is impossible (so they say). But, please, I wish people would stop trying to come up with rational-sounding and pseudo-scientific explanations for how it was all possible or how the story could possibly make any sort of sense. Just admit it was impossible and say that God can do impossible things, end of story. Stop trying to prove that your illogical and irrational beliefs are based in science and just own your beliefs for what they are.

Chapter 15.   Atheism and Evolution

As with the story of Noah's Ark described in the previous chapter, evolution and evolutionary theory are not things I would normally discuss when talking about my atheism since most theists don't find it at all controversial and there's usually nothing to discuss. However, I have run across enough Young Earth Creationists who feel the need to attack the very concept of evolution (since it apparently challenges their literal interpretation of the Biblical creation story) that I have ended up addressing the topic a few times. The following essays give my thoughts on the subject, bearing in mind that I am not an evolutionary biologist.

Atheism and Evolution

Some theists (especially those who take their scriptures extremely literally) seem to think that atheism and the theory of evolution (or "Darwinism" for those who want to imply that evolution is just some sort of cult of personality that atheists belong to based solely on faith) are inextricably linked. Apparently, either all atheists believe in evolution as their religion instead of believing in God, or else a belief in evolution is what caused people to become atheists in the first place.

In this post I want to try and unpack this a bit. First, to explain what atheism really means and what the real relationship between atheism and evolution is. And second, to try and understand why theists keep insisting on a relationship that isn't there.

First, the facts:

First of all, it's important to remember that atheism is neither a belief system nor a community of like-minded individuals. There is no official atheist doctrine, there are no appointed atheist leaders, and there are no requirements to be an atheist other than simply not believing in God. Or gods.

Second, while *many* atheists accept the Theory of Evolution by Natural Selection, not all do so and you can certainly be an atheist and not accept it. Just like you can be an atheist and think the world is flat or that aliens are regularly abducting people or that world leaders are being replaced with lizard people. Being an atheist is not the same as being a scientist or a rationalist or a materialist — it simply means that you do not believe in God. Or gods.

Third, the reason many atheists do accept the Theory of Evolution by Natural Selection is the same reason they accept, say, the theory of gravity. It's a coherent, well-established theory that explains observed phenomena that has been supported by observable evidence and is backed up by numerous other fields of study. And, keep in mind, the "theory" of evolution is the current best explanation for the observed fact of evolution, just like the "theory" of gravity is the current best explanation for the the observed fact of gravity.

Fourth, it's important to note that many **theists** also accept the theory of evolution for the same reasons many atheists do. In fact, I think it's safe to say that **most** theists accept it (although some still want to include God as the ultimate driving force behind it). The whole denial of evolution thing is really just limited to a very small number of Christians and Muslims world-wide who take their scriptures extremely literally and feel threatened by anything that could be seen to contradict those scriptures in any way (more on this later).

Finally, while it's certainly possible that *some* atheists lost their faith after learning the details of the theory of evolution (*e.g.*, because their faith was based on an assumption that God was required as an explanation for why life on earth is the way it is), the vast majority of atheists were not looking for an explanation regarding the diversity of life on earth in the first place and didn't choose to replace their religious beliefs with the "religion" of evolution. They simply lack a belief in God, whether because they were not raised to believe in God in the first place, because they were taught about God and found the notion to be rather silly, because they carefully considered the evidence for God's existence and found it lacking, or any of a thousand other reasons.

Second, the theories:

As stated above, many (if not most) theists in the world have no trouble accepting the fact that all species — including man — have evolved over long periods of time to reach their current state. They do not take their scriptures to be 100% literally true and are fine with that, focusing instead on the principles and promises made in those scriptures. A small subset of theists, however, acknowledge the hypocrisy involved in only believing in *part* of holy scriptures and therefore take an "all or nothing" approach. And, since the holy scriptures clearly state that God created man in His own image and gave him dominion over all other creatures on earth, acknowledging the fact of evolution (and accepting the validity of the current theory of evolution by natural selection) would be to deny the validity of the scriptures and the very foundation of their faith.

These theists who take their scriptures literally know full well that most of what is written in those scriptures either cannot be verified by modern science or is directly contradicted by modern science, whether it be archaeology, geology, cosmology, anthropology, physics, chemistry, biology, or what have you. But the whole concept of evolution in particular bothers them, since it undermines the whole idea of humans being uniquely special creatures in God's eyes. OK, so maybe the world wasn't *really* created 6000 years ago and maybe Noah didn't *really* have an ark full of animals and maybe Moses didn't *really* part the Red Sea, but we sure as heck didn't come from monkeys!

As a result, for those theists who take their scriptures literally and whose world view revolves around the notion that humans are special, it is only natural to assume that everybody else's world view revolves around the fundamental question of how humanity got here and what is humanity's relationship with the rest of the universe. Thus, since *their* worldview revolves around "God did it," atheists *must* have a worldview that revolves around "God didn't do it." And, since a belief that "god didn't do it" requires some alternate explanation, that explanation must be "Evolution".

So, in the eyes of these theists, it is incomprehensible that somebody could simply not believe in God (especially *their* God) without having an alternative belief system in place. And, since these theists acknowledge (whether explicitly or implicitly) that their belief system is fundamentally based on *faith* (belief without evidence or in spite of evidence to the contrary) and a reliance on the *testimony* (anecdotal stories) of others, they assume that atheist must also base their belief system on faith and testimony.

This false equivalence leads to two separate phenomena. First, there is an ongoing attempt to argue that atheism is no better than theism since both "isms" are equally reliant on "faith" and "testimony" and therefore atheists have no right to feel at all superior to theists (and theists are perfectly justified for not feeling at all inferior). Second, there is an ongoing attempt to undermine the theory of evolution in the mistaken belief that doing so will somehow convince atheists that the explanation for how humanity got here must actually be "God did it" after all.

The "Theory" of Evolution

I've lost count of how many times I've heard or seen fundamentalist theists (whether Christian or Muslim) disparage the entire concept of evolution by saying, "it's just a theory." As in, "Scientists claim that man evolved from apes, but the Theory of Evolution is just that -- a theory! It's nothing more than a guess!" I've also lost count of how many times I have heard or seen people (whether atheists or just rational theists) respond to this claim, but the responses always seem to be one of two different approaches. Some people go with a glib response to the tune of, "Evolution is 'just' a theory the same way gravity is 'just' a theory!" Others point out that the word "theory" has a different meaning when used in a scientific context than it does when used colloquially. In other words, while theory can certainly mean "simply a guess or conjecture" when used colloquially, when scientists use the term they mean "a coherent group of tested general propositions, commonly regarded as correct, that can be used as principles of explanation and prediction for a class of phenomena."

Neither of these two standard responses are particularly helpful, in my opinion. The first suffers simply because it *is* glib, and doesn't really offer enough information to change anybody's mind on the subject. Glib responses, in my experience, are best suited to making the person making the response feel superior, but don't typically have much effect on the person listening. The second response, while informative and accurate, suffers because it completely misses the entire point. It doesn't really matter if "theory" is defined to mean that it's not "just" a guess but is instead supported by evidence and generally accepted as true. That still lets fundamentalists claim that it doesn't *have* to be true. "After all," they might argue, "for centuries it was generally accepted by scientists that the earth was flat, or that the sun revolved around the earth, or that everything was made up of earth, air, fire and water."

No, I think the best response to the whole "it's just a theory" argument is to point out what the Theory of Evolution actually is, not what the word "theory" means. And no, I don't mean explain all the details of the theory and point out all the evidence that supports it (although that can certainly be helpful if you have the scientific background to pull it off). I'm talking about something a lot more basic which always seems to get missed in these discussions. It is important to explain that the Theory of Evolution is *not* the proposition that there is such a thing as evolution in the first place, that all currently existing species (including man) have evolved from previously existing species, and that all life on earth shares a common ancestor who lived billions of years ago. Instead, the Theory of Evolution is the proposition to explain how and why all of that took place.

Evolution, in other words, is an observable, demonstrable **fact** and not a theory at all! The Theory of Evolution is our best explanation (supported by evidence and commonly accepted as accurate) as to what caused (and still causes) that fact. And just because our best explanation *might* be incomplete or inaccurate or just flat-out wrong doesn't say anything about whether scientists are at all unsure as to whether evolution is a real thing. This is similar to how the "Theory of Gravity" does not seek to explain whether or not there *is* gravity, but instead seeks to explain *why* there is gravity and *how* it works.

Evolution is an observable and demonstrable fact, plain and simple. We have a multitude of evidence from various sources, such as the fossil record, comparative anatomy, DNA analysis, etc., that shows unequivocally that all life on earth has evolved from prior life forms over time and that all living creatures shared common ancestors in the past. Evolution itself is not a theory -- it's simply an observation. The Theory of Evolution deals with *how* and *why* evolution occurred and the commonly accepted explanation is that evolution is caused by the occurrence of random mutations within a population that gives rise to variety, and that changes in environment cause different variations within the population to either thrive or perish, which over vast time scales can lead to entirely new species, genera, orders, classes, phyla and even kingdoms.

Whether this theory is wholly accurate and complete can certainly be discussed. It is, after all, "just" a coherent group of tested genera propositions, commonly regarded as correct, that can be used as principles of explanation and prediction. Maybe there are additional factors at work that we haven't figured out yet. Maybe some of the factors we currently believe to be involved aren't as important as we think. Maybe we've got it completely wrong and there is a totally different explanation for how evolution has occurred (and is still occurring). Maybe that explanation is even "God did it" (or "aliens did it" or "magic pixies did it"). But none of that uncertainty changes the fact that evolution has occurred and continues to occur.

Evolution is a fact. The explanation as to how it works is a theory. A very good, commonly accepted theory that can be and has been used as principles of explanation and prediction, but a theory nonetheless. And this, I believe, is the best response to the whole "evolution is just a theory" argument. Yes, the "Theory of Evolution" is a theory, but evolution itself is an accepted, observable, demonstrable fact.

Accepting Evolution

Although the theory of evolution doesn't really have anything to do with Atheism, *per se*, it often comes up in discussions with theists who apparently feel threatened by something which can so fully explain observable phenomena that theists have been claiming for centuries could only be explained by the existence of a divine creator. Before the theory of evolution was proposed (and, eventually, accepted), there just wasn't any good way to explain the immense diversity of life on earth and the way it is all so interconnected. Of course, claiming that God "must" have done it since we can't think of any other explanation is a classic "Argument from Ignorance," but the fact remained that there were no other decent explanations for a long time. With the theory of evolution, however, you no longer need God to explain everything, and this has led some theists to attempt to undermine its acceptance at every opportunity. Not all theist, mind you -- the Catholic Church, for example, officially recognizes the science behind the theory of evolution and "merely" claims that God directed the process and at some point in that process injected the human soul into the mix.

Somebody once asked me asked whether it was possible to come up with grand unifying analogy or quote to fully explain the theory of evolution and make it more understandable and accepted by those who deny it. Unfortunately, while analogies may be useful in *understanding* the general concepts underlying evolution, I don't think they are much use when it comes to actually *accepting* the truth of evolution. And this is the case with most fields of science that attempt to explain things that are not, and cannot, be perceived directly and which may even appear to contradict our everyday experiences.

Relativity, for example, is truly weird, especially when you talk about curved space/time. Sure, comparing space/time to a rubber sheet and massive objects to a bowling ball rolling along that sheet may help me understand the general idea that somebody is talking about, but at the end of the day it doesn't really help me to understand what space/time really is or accept that it can be somehow distorted by massive objects. That will only come by learning a lot of complex mathematics and performing (or at least studying) tons of experiments. And if I insisted that all theories that describe reality must comport with my "common sense" view of the world, I would never be able to accept the validity of relativity, despite the fact that it is widely accepted among physicists and is actually used on a daily basis for such things as making adjustments to GPS satellites that are further away from the Earth's gravitational pull and therefore run at a slightly different speed than clocks on earth. Seriously weird stuff, but also seriously true.

Quantum mechanics is even worse. It has been said that nobody truly understands it, and yet its principals have been borne out by experimentation and physicists can make accurate predictions based on the various laws that have been discovered regarding it. Of course, the world we can observe with our eyes and ears does not operate on the quantum level, and once again my "common sense" experiences are not a reliable means of judging the validity of quantum mechanics.

Like relativity and quantum mechanics, the theory of evolution describes reality as it occurs on a scale not generally observable by our standard senses. In the case of evolution, the scale has to do with time rather than size or speed or distance. And, just like relativity and quantum mechanics, we cannot rely on our own "common sense" experiences as a guide to determining whether or not it is an accurate description of reality. Once again, however, just like the theories of relativity and quantum mechanics, the theory of evolution provides an explanation as to why the universe behaves the way it does and also lets us make falsifiable predictions as to what will happen in the future.

To understand evolution, all you really need to know (and I hope I'm getting this right) is that (a) small, random changes are occurring all the time within all biological organisms due to such things as random cosmic ray bombardment and the fact that organisms generally get a random distribution of different genes from each "parent", (b) the environment in which most organisms live is constantly changing as well (either due to a change in the environment itself or because the organisms have moved to a different environment), and (c) these two factors frequently combine so that some members of any given species find themselves better suited to the current environment (and thereby survive to pass on their genes to future generations) while other members of that species find themselves less suited (and thereby do not survive to pass on their genes to future generations). Add to that a time span of millions and even billions of years for small changes to accumulate, *et voila*!

The best analogy I have read to help me accept the truth of the theory evolution is the one described in Richard Dawkin's "Climbing Mount Improbable." It doesn't lend itself to a pithy quote, unfortunately, but the general analogy compares the evolution of, say, mammals from their ancient fish-like ancestors to a sheer-faced cliff hundreds (thousands?) of feet high. To somebody standing at the base of the cliff, the very thought of leaping to the top in a single bound is impossible to consider, just like it may be impossible to imagine a fish turning into a mouse. But, the analogy continues, what if you could look at the other side of the cliff and see a gradual slope extending for tens (or even hundreds) of miles in the distance leading from sea level all the way to the cliff's edge? If you started a journey from the very beginning of the slope, the incline would be so gradual that at no point in your journey would you ever even notice you were rising. You could travel for days, weeks, months and still appear to be traveling on perfectly level ground. And yet, at the end of your journey you would eventually find yourself thousands of feet in the air despite never having made any perceptible leaps whatsoever. Replace "hundreds of miles" in the cliff analogy with "millions of years" in the theory of evolution, and the analogy is complete. The analogy only works, however, if you fully understand the processes involved with evolution in the first place.

Hopefully, this analogy provides with a framework to understand how evolution is even possible, similar to how the bowling ball on a rubber sheet analogy might help somebody understand the concept of warped space. It's not an exact analogy, but it should help (assuming, of course, that somebody actually *wants* to understand how evolution could possibly be true instead of just rejecting it out of hand). Having said that, let me just address a few of the most common criticisms I have seen and heard lobbed at evolution by those who clearly do not understand how it could be possible:

If humans evolved from apes, why are there still apes around today?

This is an easy one to answer -- humans did not evolve from apes! At least, not from the apes that are around today. Instead, humans and apes both evolved from a common ancestor species millions of years ago and we turned out different from modern apes because we moved to different locations than they did, encountered different challenges than they did, faced different environments over time, etc. It's sort of like asking, "If the English language evolved from Germanic roots, why are there still German speaking people today?"

If evolution is true, why don't we ever find any "transitional" fossils that are clearly in between two other species?

The answer to this is that scientists have actually found many different transitional fossils, especially in recent years. Numerous fossils have been found in the fossil record that show some characteristics of fossils found earlier in the fossil record and some characteristics of fossils found later in the fossil record. The problem is that some people either are not aware of these discoveries (willful ignorance, perhaps) or require impossible standards for "transitional" like a fossil that is half duck and half crocodile, despite the fact that the theory of evolution clearly states that evolution is a gradual process with no sudden leaps from one species to a wholly unrelated species on in a single generation. No duck ever gave birth to an animal that wasn't a duck, but over millions of years what is a duck now may be quite different from what was a duck back then.

If evolution is true, that means we are just animals and therefore have no reason to act morally toward one another.

Well, aside from the fact that this is basically arguing from the consequences (a logical fallacy where you try to disprove something simply by pointing out the possible negative consequences of that thing), I would have to take exception at the "just" part of this criticism. True, evolution means that humans are animals, but why do we have to be "just" animals? A dolphin is not "just" an animal -- it is an animal with a highly specialized, perhaps unique, ability to navigate underwater using sound. An eagle is not "just" an animal -- it's an animal with exceedingly keen vision and the ability to soar through the sky. And man is not "just" an animal, either -- he (or she) is an animal with a highly developed intelligence and moral sense that has evolved over time to help us better survive in our environment. The fact that we are animals doesn't mean we can't be different from other animals in significant ways, and it certainly doesn't mean that we have to *act* like other animals any more than you would expect an eagle to act like a dolphin (or to act like a penguin, for that matter).

Evolution is just a "theory" that Darwin made up and scientists have blindly put their faith in it ever since!

Actually, no. As mentioned above, the scientific use of the word "theory" (as in the "theory of gravity" and the "theory of relativity") is used to describe a system of interrelated laws and principles that have been **tested**, **validated** and **confirmed** and that are used to describe a particular area of observed reality. Darwin (and others like him) may have first proposed the idea of natural selection being the primary driver for observed evolutionary changes, but it didn't become a scientific "theory" until it had been thoroughly tested, revised, expanded upon, and confirmed by generations of scientists looking at many different fields for corroboration. In addition, it's important to realize that evolution itself is actually an observed fact. The "theory" of evolution is our best explanation for how and when it occurs, not that it occurs in the first place.

The odds of a complex organism like a human arising purely by "chance" are as ridiculous as a tornado whipping through a junkyard and assembling a complete, working jumbo jet airplane purely by chance!

You're right, that would be rather ridiculous. But the theory of evolution doesn't actually state that everything happened purely by chance. Yes, it requires chance mutations to occur and accumulate over time, but that's just an ingredient in the recipe and not the recipe itself. The actual process of evolution is driven by the pressure of natural selection. It may be chance when one animal develops more hair than another member of the same species, but it's not chance when that hairier animal survives when the climate gets colder and the less hairy animal doesn't.

Evolution can't explain how life got started in the first place.

You're right, it can't. But, then again, neither can the theory of gravity or the theory of relativity. And that's because none of those theories actually *claim* to answer that question and their validity therefore does not rest on whether they can answer it or not. There is a completely separate field of biology called **Abiogenesis** that *does* try to come up with theories to explain how life could first arise (whether from inanimate matter or some other way, such as having been carried to Earth on a comet). Evolution, on the other hand, starts with the assumption that life exists and then explains how it became so diverse. For more thoughts on this, see *Addressing Arguments Against Abiogenesis* on p.218.

But, what about [insert anomaly mentioned exclusively on creationist websites that seemingly "disproves" some tangentially related principal]?

I don't have room to mention every single thing that creationists have come up with over the years in an attempt to "disprove" evolution. The important thing to remember, however, is that not only does evolution stand as the best explanation ever devised for every bit of observed biological phenomena, and not only has it shown again and again that it has strong predictive powers, it is also corroborated by many other branches of science. If the theory of evolution were just based on the observed fossil record, then maybe attacking the validity of the fossil record could be an attack on the theory itself. Instead, though, the theory of evolution is based on corroborating observations from the fossil record, from comparative physiology, from the genetic analysis of living species, from field examinations of species evolving in the wild, etc.

But, there's no actual proof of evolution!

Oh, go read a book. No, seriously. Preferably one written by an actual scientist with a degree from a real university with a degree in a field actually related to the study of evolution. That is, of course, if you actually want to learn all about the proof instead of just repeating what others have told you. Creationists have been shouting "there's no proof of evolution" for over a hundred years, ignoring or dismissing every single bit of evidence that comes along, as if simply stating that something isn't true will somehow make it not true. Or, in other words, yes there *is* actual proof of the theory of evolution. Lots of proof. So much proof that it could (and actually does) fill entire libraries. You just have to be willing to look at it.

Another Evolution Analogy

As mentioned earlier, Richard Dawkins' "Climbing Mount Improbable" includes a wonderful analogy comparing the gradual process of evolution to a walk up a very gradual slope that eventually leads to the top of a very high mountain. It's a very good analogy, but I fear it may require a bit too much work to accept it since (a) not everybody has experience with climbing up gradual slopes and (b) a change in altitude is not really in the same conceptual ballpark as the change that species undergo over time. Its strength is, I believe, primarily in the way it conveys how extremely small changes can add up to large changes over extreme lengths of time. But some folks will probably still reject it because they simply can't get their minds wrapped around the comparison of time to distance.

After much thought, I believe I have come up with, if not a *better* analogy, at least a *complimentary* analogy to the one Professor Dawkins discussed. It lacks the sense of vast time in Dawkins' analogy, but is more grounded in everyday experience and deals with actual biological processes. It also helps deal with the common objection heard by Creationists that there are no "transitional" fossils that show one species evolving into a completely different species.

Let's imagine a father who photographs his newborn child and decides to take a new photograph of the child once every minute of every hour of every single day from that point on. At the end of the first day, the father has 1400 pictures, after one week he has 10,080 pictures, and at the end of a year he has a whopping 525,960 pictures. At the end of ten years, the stack has grown to 5,259,600 pictures, and by the time the child is 50 years old, the stack has grown to 26,298,000 pictures. And (assuming the father was extremely long-lived or passed the duties on to somebody else), by the time the child is 90 years old, the stack has a massive 47,336,400 pictures, all showing the gradual growth of a baby into an elderly man one minute at a time.

Now, over a period of ninety years, the child has changed from a newborn infant to an elderly man, and along the way the child progressed through various well-defined stages (infant, toddler, child, pre-teen, adolescent, young adult, adult, middle-age, senior citizen, elderly) . And if you randomly selected any example from that stack of 47,336,400 pictures, you would be able to clearly identify which stage of life the child was in at the time that photograph was taken. No photograph, however, would show a clear "transition" from one stage to the next. You wouldn't, for example, find a picture showing the child with the body of a baby and the head of a toddler. Or the arms of a teenager but the legs of an adult. Or (to mirror some of the extreme examples asked for by Young Earth Creationists), the body of an infant and the head of a senior citizen.

The point is that the change from infant to elder is so gradual that there are no clear-cut transitions from one stage of life to the next. Somebody may legally be considered an adult at the age of 18, but it would be impossible to detect any physiological differences between a person one minute or one hour or even day *before* his 18th birthday and one minute, hour or day *after* his 18th birthday. And this isn't to say that there aren't any transitional photographs of the child; instead, it means that *every single photograph shows a transition from the previous minute to the next minute* and the supposedly "well-defined" stages of life are really just shortcuts we use to describe people instead of actually having some sort of absolute definitions.

The same is generally true with regard to the fossil record and the evidence it provides for evolutionary processes. Just as children gradually change into adults over time, species gradually change into other species over time. The only difference is that species change over millions of years instead of 90 years, but the principal is the same. Just as you will never find a photograph of somebody who has the head of an infant and the body of an adult, you will never find a fossil showing the head of one species and the body of a previous species. And this isn't to say that there aren't any transitional fossils; instead, it means that *every single fossil shows a transition from the prior generation to the following generation* and the concept of "well-defined" species is really just a shortcut we use to describe life instead of actually having some sort of absolute definition.

Evolution and Why Labels Don't Matter

Theists (especially Young Earth Creationists who deny the reality of evolution) love to make a big deal about the emergence of species, constantly asking for evidence of one species (or "kind") turning into another, or asking how the "first" member of a species could have possibly shown up suddenly one day if it had no other member of its species to mate with, etc. Here's the thing that these folks either do not understand or else choose to ignore, however:

We humans looooove labels. We just can't help ourselves. We have this innate burning need to distinguish everything from everything else and give it all labels to make sure that everybody knows what we are talking about. We have chairs and we have beds. When somebody invents something that can be used as both a chair and a bed, we call it a futon rather than just admitting that "chair" and "bed" are arbitrary labels in the first place. We label eating utensils that have tines as "forks" and eating utensils that have bowl-like depressions as "spoons". But then somebody comes up with a utensil that has tines *and* a bowl-like depression, and we have to come up with a new label "spork" (or "runcible spoon," if you prefer) because we just can't deal with something that contradicts our previously defined labels.

The same is true with biology. We have "cats" and we have "dogs" and we have "birds" and we somehow think that just because we have come up with these labels that nature somehow cares one whit about making sure that reality conforms with them. And, sure, it's pretty obvious that cats and dogs and birds are pretty distinct from each other, but things get awfully muddy when you start labeling each individual species of cat, dog and bird. Not to mention ape. We have arbitrarily defined "species" as groups of animals that can interbreed with each other, but this is simply our way of labeling things and not a hard and fast natural law. That's why there are things like "ring species" where one group of animals can interbreed with a similar group living in proximity to them, and that group can interbreed with another group that lives in proximity to them, etc., but you eventually get to a group that can interbreed with their closest neighbor but cannot interbreed with the original group. We then feel compelled to label the last group a different species from the first group.

All of this is to say that, yes, evolution is true and occurring all the time and yes, this means that any labels we put on things with regard to species, genus, etc., are necessarily going to be imprecise and have gray areas and be subject to revision. Which is, of course, why it is so ironic when some people who deny evolution claim it's impossible for one "kind" of animal to evolve into another "kind" over time, as if they themselves have some infallible way of labeling things.

Chapter 16.   Addressing Arguments Against Abiogensis

[Sorry, just couldn't resist the alliteration.]

Abiogenesis is the concept of life arising from nonliving matter ("biogenesis" is defined as "the production of living organisms from other living organisms" and the "a-" prefix simply means "not"). And it's a concept that frequently gets attacked by fundamentalist theists as part of a larger attack against "evolutionists," "scientists" and/or "atheists" (which fundamentalists tend to all lump together since they apparently can't imagine a theist actually accepting any scientific thought or discovery that contradicts their literal interpretation of their own particular holy book, but I digress). These attacks usually take one or more of the following forms:

"Abiogenesis is just impossible. It's ridiculous to think that nonliving matter could ever produce living matter, there is no evidence that such a thing is even possible and certainly no evidence that it actually happened."

"The Theory of Evolution doesn't explain how life originally originated on Earth, so therefore the entire theory is flawed."

"Science has already established that life cannot come from non-life — Louis Pasteur disproved the doctrine of the "spontaneous generation" of life well over 100 years ago."

"Atheists think that one day a rock just turned into a complex living being after it was struck by lightning."

Now, I am not any sort of biologist and am therefore not qualified to present the evidence we currently have that shows that abiogenesis is possible or the current theories that explain exactly how it might have happened. Instead, allow me to present some philosophical (dare I say "common sense"?) responses to these various attacks that you might find useful (especially when faced with creationists who refuse to consider the actual evidence).

"Abiogenesis is just impossible. It's ridiculous to think that nonliving matter could ever produce living matter, there is no evidence that such a thing is even possible and certainly no evidence that it actually happened."

The response to this is that abiogenesis is not only *possible*, it actually *must* have happened. It's a philosophical certainty, in fact. After all, we now know that the entire universe began to expand from an initially very hot and very dense state some 13.7 billion years ago and that the first simple molecules of helium hydride didn't appear until around 100,000 years after that initial expansion began. Therefore, we know that at some point in the distant past there could not have possibly been any life whatsoever in the universe and that therefore life *must* have somehow arisen from the nonliving matter that did exist.

The only question is when and how it happened, of course. Even most fundamentalist theists believe that it happened, although they tend to think it happened some 6,000–10,000 years in the past and involved a deity of some sort creating life out of the dust of the earth or clay or what have you. But you can't simultaneously claim that abiogenesis is impossible and then describe how your deity did it.

"The Theory of Evolution doesn't explain how life originally originated on Earth, so therefore the entire theory is flawed."

The Theory of Evolution explains how the observed scientific fact of evolution takes place and has nothing whatsoever to do with explaining where life on Earth first came from. It also doesn't try to explain what existed prior to the so-called "Big Bang" or how photons exhibit a particle/wave duality or why time appears to slow down inside a gravity well. Criticizing a theory for not explaining something it isn't even meant to explain in the first place is just perverse.

More importantly, though, the Theory of Evolution has done a *very, very* good job at explaining how the observed scientific fact of evolution takes place. Even if its inability to explain the origin of life were somehow a "gap" or "hole" in the theory, that would simply mean that the theory was *incomplete*, not that it was therefore completely false, disproved, discredited, or what have you.

I always find it stunningly hypocritical, by the way, when fundamentalist theists claim that if *any* part of the Theory of Evolution can be shown to be at all incorrect in any way whatsoever, the entire theory is therefore invalidated. Because, of course, the same doesn't hold true when it comes to their deeply held religious beliefs.

"Science has already established that life cannot come from non-life — Louis Pasteur disproved the doctrine of the "spontaneous generation" of life well over 100 years ago."

Yes, it is true that Louis Pasteur disproved the doctrine of "spontaneous generation" of life way back in the 1860s. But "spontaneous generation" is not actually the same thing as "abiogenesis" and it's incredibly disingenuous (not to mention frankly dishonest) to attempt to conflate those two concepts in this context.

Spontaneous generation specifically refers to the outdated idea that **ordinary complex living organisms** could form from inanimate matter without descending from similar existing organisms. Not only that, but the process of living creatures arising from nonliving matter was commonplace and regular and could explain how fleas seemingly appeared from nowhere ("they are generated from inanimate dust") or how maggots suddenly appeared on dead flesh ("the dead flesh itself created them").

Pasteur disproved this idea through various experiments involving things like covering up dead flesh with a glass lid and observing that no maggots appeared and later scientists were able to actually observe fleas and flies laying their eggs to further disprove the idea. But that has precisely nothing whatsoever to do with the proposed process by which the first **extremely simple** life forms first came to exist (under conditions that perhaps only existed billions of years ago and would therefore not be at all commonplace and regular).

"Atheists think that one day a rock just turned into a complex living being after it was struck by lightning."

Actually, nobody thinks this. Feel free to check out the links I provided earlier, but current thinking is that abiogenesis occurred over a relatively long period of time and involved numerous "precursors" such as amino acids and lipids and other such things being formed independently and eventually coming together to form complicated molecules that eventually became the precursor to what we now know as RNA. And even then, that wouldn't exactly have been "life as we know it" but would have continued to develop over time until finally becoming something "fully" alive by modern definitions of the term.

And many of these precursors, including rudimentary amino acids, have actually been produced in laboratory conditions from inanimate materials, indicating that the formation of life might actually be an inevitability given the proper conditions due to the simple operation of chemistry.

A large part of the resistance to this idea of the gradual formation of life from nonliving matter comes, I think, from an assumption that there is a clear distinction between "life" and "non-life" and that it doesn't matter how close inanimate matter may *appear* to be alive if it doesn't have that undefinable "spark of life" (that can only come from God, of course). But that's only if you choose to limit your consideration to complex life forms that are clearly alive. It's hard to argue, for example, that your typical slime mold acts much like a living organism despite the fact that we know they are alive. More to the point, viruses are generally considered to *not* be alive despite the fact that they exhibit *some* traits that we typically associate with living organisms.

All of which is to say that the earliest forms of "life" that first emerged here on Earth likely bore little resemblance to anything we would consider "alive" today, which is not at all surprising given the fact that that early life has had billions of years to evolve since then.

It's not that surprising that fundamentalist theists tend to think of life in such stark "life/non-life" terms, of course, since they tend to think that is how their particular deity did things. Take a bunch of clay, breathe "spirit" into it, and *voila*! The first human being. Absolutely and utterly impossible, right? Well, unless you happen to believe in deity that just so happens to be conveniently defined as having the ability to do impossible things…

Chapter 17.   On the Lighter Side

The Holy Note Paper of Barry

The following is a humorous response to the claim made by some Christians that the Bible is the infallible, perfect word of God, which we can know is true because it says so right there in the Bible. Oh — and we know that God is infallible and incapable of lying because it says that in the Bible as well. So if we know the Bible is true because it is the word of God, and we know it is the word of God because the Bible says it is…

Behold, the Holy Note Paper of Barry:

THE NOTE PAPER OF BARRY

1. Behold, this is the Note Paper of Barry.
2. For verily, it was written by Barry.
3. Now, I say unto you that Barry is All-powerful, All-knowing and utterly infallible.
4. Yea, and everything written by Him is completely true.
5. "But," the fool might ask in his heart, "how can I know that Barry is All-powerful, All-knowing and utterly infallible"?
6. Behold! This Note Paper says He is, and everything written on this Note Paper is completely true.
7. "But," the unwise might ask in his heart, "how can I know that everything written on this Note Paper is completely true"?
8. Verily, I say unto you, this Note Paper was written by Barry, who is All-powerful, All-knowing and utterly infallible.

1. *Behold, this is the Note Paper of Barry.*
2. *For verily, it was written by Barry.*
3. *Now, I say unto you that Barry is all-powerful, all-knowing and utterly infallible.*
4. *Yea, and everything written by Him is completely true.*
5. *"But," the fool might ask in his heart, "how can I know that Barry is all-powerful, all-knowing and utterly infallible"?*
6. *Behold! This Note Paper says He is, and everything written on this Note Paper is completely true.*
7. *"But," the unwise might ask in his heart, "how can I know that everything written on this Note Paper is completely true"?*
8. *Verily, I say unto you, this Note Paper was written by Barry, who is all-powerful, all-knowing and utterly infallible.*

After the words of Barry were originally set down upon the Holy Note Paper of Barry, it came to my attention that some Christians go so far as to claim that there is actually no such thing as an atheist in the first place, since the Bible supposedly says (in Romans 1:18-23, apparently) that everybody secretly knows that God exists. All right, then! Time for a little latter-day revelation, I guess:

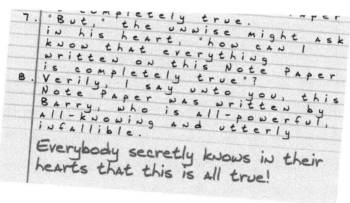

The Prophecies of the One True God, Bob McDobbitt

Every once in a while, I encounter a Christian who claims that Jesus Christ *must* be God because his life fulfilled many different prophecies made in the Old Testament (as many as 300 separate prophecies by some accounts). Usually, it's easy enough to point out that many of the supposed "prophecies" are either extremely vague or else don't seem to actually have anything to do with the coming of a Messiah (or even be prophecies in the first place — the mention of Aaron, the brother of Moses, raising up a staff, for example, really can't be considered a "prophecy" that the Messiah would be raised up on a cross unless you are particularly desperate). But that gets a little tedious after a while as every prophecy you debunk will be countered by, "Well, what about *this* one?" Just one big game of Whack-a-Mole, you know?

However, regardless of how vague these prophecies are or whether they are even prophecies to begin with, it's important to remember that all we really have here are *stories* written down that claim to be a true history of actual events with no verification. The people who wrote the stories contained in the New Testament about the life of Jesus (many decades after Jesus himself supposedly lived and died) surely were familiar with the Tanakh (the Hebrew Bible that formed the basis of the Old Testament), being most likely Jewish themselves. And they most likely knew of various prophecies that could be interpreted to refer to the coming Messiah. As a result, it's not much of a stretch to think that they actually made-up details of Jesus's life specifically to make it seem as though some of those prophecies were fulfilled.

In other words, it's easy for somebody to have fulfilled previously written prophecies if the people writing the story of his life are aware of those prophecies and make up the details of the person's life to fit. How easy? Allow me to demonstrate…

Here is a list of seven very specific prophecies telling people about the coming of the One True God:

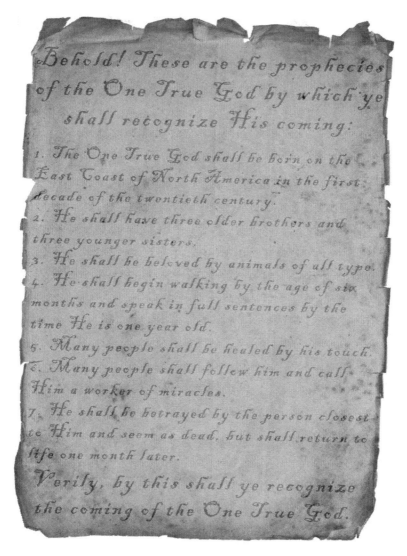

Behold! These are the prophecies of the One True God by which ye shall recognize His coming:

1. The One True God shall be born on the East Coast of North America in the first decade of the twentieth century.
2. He shall have three older brothers and three younger sisters.
3. He shall be beloved by animals of all type.
4. He shall begin walking by the age of six months and speak in full sentences by the time He is one year old.
5. Many people shall be healed by his touch.
6. Many people shall follow him and call Him a worker of miracles.
7. He shall be betrayed by the person closest to Him and seem as dead, but shall return to life one month later.

Verily, by this shall ye recognize the coming of the One True God.

And here, written at a later time, is the story of one man who actually fulfilled each and every one of those very specific prophecies:

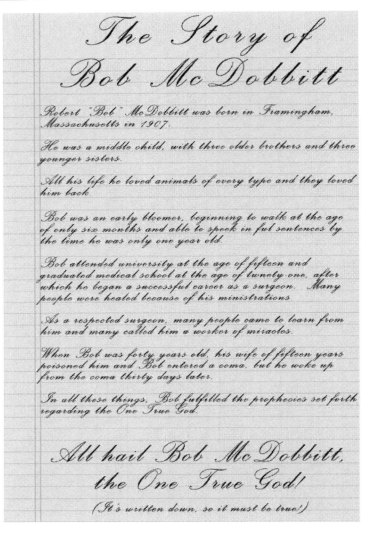

The Story of
Bob McDobbitt

Robert "Bob" McDobbitt was born in Framingham, Massachusetts in 1907.

He was a middle child, with three older brothers and three younger sisters.

All his life he loved animals of every type and they loved him back.

Bob was an early bloomer, beginning to walk at the age of only six months and able to speak in full sentences by the time he was only one year old.

Bob attended university at the age of fifteen and graduated medical school at the age of twenty-one, after which he began a successful career as a surgeon. Many people were healed because of his ministrations.

As a respected surgeon, many people came to learn from him and many called him a worker of miracles.

When Bob was forty years old, his wife of fifteen years poisoned him and Bob entered a coma, but he woke up from the coma thirty days later.

In all these things, Bob fulfilled the prophecies set forth regarding the One True God.

All hail Bob McDobbitt, the One True God!

(It's written down, so it must be true!)

The bottom line is that it's not all that impressive when one fictional book contains stories that supposedly fulfills prophecies made in a previous fictional book.

ALL HAIL BOB MCDOBBITT!

Atheism in Iambic Tetrameter

For some reason, people keep asking me whether I believe in God or not. Usually I just say "no," but one particular time I decided to have a little fun and present my answer in iambic tetrameter (with sincerest apologies to Dr. Seuss, from whom I learned my craft as a wayward youth):

> *I do not believe in the God of the Jew.*
> *The Christian God is fictitious, too.*
> *I cannot accept that Allah is God,*
> *And the Hindu deities are just way too flawed.*
> *The ancient Egyptian gods are not real,*
> *Nor are the Greek and Roman, I feel.*
> *Sumerian gods are all just right out.*
> *And the Celtic gods? They have no clout.*
> *Thor and Odin and the other Aesir?*
> *I just don't think they're really here.*
> *The Aborigines have their own pantheon,*
> *But all of it's rubbish! Oh boy, this is fun!*
> *What of the Mayans and Aztecs and such?*
> *Well, their gods don't excite me too much.*
> *Buddha's not a god, so he doesn't count,*
> *And the Asian gods will never be found.*
> *The list could go on, there are thousands to go,*
> *But I've made my point, as I'm sure you all know.*
> *It's all superstition and none of it's true!*
> *You can pray all you like 'til your face turns bright blue.*
> *Gods are made up, every single last one.*
> *That's what I believe, and now I am done.*

Of Gods and Nigerian Princes

Have you ever received an email from somebody claiming to be, say, the widow of a Nigerian prince or a Nigerian minister of finance? You know, one of those e-mails telling you that they desperately need your help to move a staggering sum of money out of the country, and in return for your help they would be happy to split the money with you? All they need is a little money up front to pay for some paperwork…

Now, if you have received one of these emails, perhaps you were gullible enough to actually believe that the widow of a Nigerian prince would reach out to you, of all the people in the world. Or perhaps you felt it was possibly or even probably a scam, but the amount of money being asked for up front was pretty small and the potential reward was so great that you felt it was worth the risk. And so, you sent in your money. After which, of course, you received another email requesting more money to help bribe some officials. And then another email asking for even more money to pay some additional unexpected custom fees. And then another e-mail asking for even more money, until you finally realized that this was most definitely a scam and you had just wasted thousands of your hard-earned dollars.

More likely, though, you probably weren't gullible enough to take the email at face value. You were probably smart enough to realize that the odds of an actual widow of a Nigerian prince reaching out to you, of all people, was so small as to be essentially nonexistent. Perhaps you had heard of other people falling for this scam before. Perhaps you had read news reports about how common these scams are and that such emails are always scams. Perhaps you have received so many different variations of the same email that you finally realized, while they can't all be true, they can certainly all be false.

Regardless of whether you initially believed the e-mail until finally coming to your senses or whether you believed it to be a scam right from the beginning, at some point you became convinced that no member of Nigerian royalty was ever going to offer to share $50 million with you, right? Does it matter that there is theoretically a *possibility* (regardless of how small) that one of those e-mails might actually be legitimate? Does it matter that the potential reward is huge if one of those e-mails actually were true? Is there anything that could change your mind that these e-mails are all scams? And, if not, how would you respond to somebody who accused you of being "dogmatic" in your conviction that all such e-mails are scams?

Theism is a scam.

It promises huge rewards for seemingly little time, effort and/or money on our part (which effort often grows over time as we get more and more invested in the idea), but offers no actual evidence to support it. And the very idea is ludicrous and contrary to observed reality to begin with. Some atheists started out believing in a god before finally coming to their senses, while others knew enough to see it for the scam it was from the beginning. But neither of those things makes an atheist "dogmatic" in their disbelief, any more than recognizing that an e-mail purportedly from the widow of a Nigerian prince is a scam makes you "dogmatic" in your disbelief.

> *My Dearest Friend,*
>
> *Permit me to inform you of my desire of entering into a relationship with you. I have the believe you are a reputable and responsible and trustworthy person I can have a relationship with from the little information so far I gathered about you during my search for a beneficiary and by matter of trust I must not hesitate to confide in you for this simple and sincere relationship.*
>
> *I am Jesus Christ, the only begotten son of the Yahweh (also called Jehovah, Elohim, Adonai, or just plain God) who was*

worshiped by a small group of nomadic desert tribesmen some 3000 years ago. My father has a beautiful mansion and more wealth than he can ever possibly use, so he sent me to let people know that they could go live with him if they wanted to forever and ever in a state of eternal bliss.

Dearest one, in the capacity of Yahweh's only living heir and with all the documents in my hand now, I am contacting you with due sence of humanity that you will give it a sympathetic and mutual consideration.I am honourably seeking your assistance in the following ways.

(1) To serve as an ambassador to spread the word that my father wants to share his wealth with everybody.

(2) To make arrangement for me to return to the Earth to further my mission.

(3) To build up my father's organization here on the Earth.

Moreover, I am willing to offer you your very own reserved spot in my father's glorious mansion as compensation for your effort /input after the successful work performed by you on my behalf during your life.and I have mapped numerous blessings "whatsoever you ask for") for any expenses that might be incured during the course of this transaction.

Furthermore, you can indicate your option towards assisting me as I believe that this transaction would be concluded within a stipulated period of time you signify your interest to assist me.

Anticipating hearing from you immediately.

Thanks and Yahweh bless.

Jesus Christ

The Ongoing Adventures of "Maude and Eugene"™

The Ongoing Adventures of Maude and Eugene features a devout theist who thinks he has all the answers and his long-suffering wife who enjoys bursting his bubble at every opportunity. Sure, it's a dysfunctional marriage, but it's a fun way to point out the common-sense responses to many of the assertions made by some theists.

"Arrogance"

"Belief #1"

"Belief #2"

"Belief System #1"

"Belief System #2"

The Ongoing Adventures of "Maude and Eugene" ™

THE "BIG BANG" THEORY IS SCIENTIFIC PROOF THAT GOD CREATED THE UNIVERSE BY SAYING

LET THERE BE LIGHT

JUST LIKE IT SAYS IN THE BIBLE!

Yes, dear. Except, of course, for the fact that the so-called "big bang" theory doesn't actually describe the formation of the universe and instead just describes the beginning of a transition from a very hot and dense state to a cooler and less dense state.

And it took place nearly 14 billion years ago, not 6000 years.

And the first visible light wouldn't have been appeared for hundreds of thousands of years after the initial expansion.

COMMON SENSE ATHEISM

"Big Bang"

The Ongoing Adventures of "Maude and Eugene" ™

THE "CAMBRIAN EXPLOSION" IS SCIENTIFIC PROOF THAT GOD CREATED ALL LIFE ON EARTH AT ONCE, JUST LIKE IT SAYS IN THE BIBLE!

Yes, dear. Except, of course, according to science the "Cambrian Explosion" describes a period of 13–27 million years that happened some 541 million years ago when the first animals that had bodies hard enough to regularly become fossilized gradually began to appear on the earth.

Oh – and not a single species alive today existed back then. No cats, no dogs, no horses, no camels, no sheep, no pigs, etc. In fact, there were no birds, no fish, no reptiles and no mammals. Just a bunch of very early forms of animal life that were just starting to develop hard shells.

COMMON SENSE ATHEISM

"Cambrian"

"Circular"

"Creation"

"Deluded"

"Design"

The Ongoing Adventures of "Maude and Eugene" ™

ALBERT EINSTEIN BELIEVED IN GOD! DO ATHEISTS THINK THEY ARE SMARTER THAN EINSTEIN?

Yes, dear. And I'm sure that's why Einstein wrote, "The word God is for me nothing more than the expression and product of human weaknesses, the Bible a collection of honourable, but still primitive legends."

"Einstein"

The Ongoing Adventures of "Maude and Eugene" ™

THE SECOND LAW OF THERMODYNAMICS SAYS THAT ENTROPY CAN NEVER DECREASE OVER TIME. THEREFORE, EVOLUTION IS IMPOSSIBLE SINCE IT CLAIMS THAT LIFE HAS BECOME MORE COMPLEX OVER TIME!

Yes, dear. Except, of course, if you actually read a science book instead of relying on creationist websites, you'd know that the second law only applies to "isolated" systems instead of systems like the Earth that constantly get extra energy from the sun.

COMMON SENSE ATHEISM

"Entropy"

The Ongoing Adventures of "Maude and Eugene" ™

THERE IS SOOOOOOO MUCH EVIDENCE THAT PROVES GOD EXISTS, INCLUDING STORIES OF MIRACLES, PERSONAL SPIRITUAL WITNESSES, AND THE FACT THAT SCIENCE CAN'T EXPLAIN EVERYTHING!

Yes, dear. Of course, it's odd that you wouldn't accept any of that sort of evidence as proof of anything else *other* than the existence of the particular god you believe in...

COMMON SENSE ATHEISM

"Evidence #1"

The Ongoing Adventures of "Maude and Eugene" ™

I DON'T JUST BELIEVE IN GOD – I KNOW HE EXISTS! PLUS, I KNOW EXACTLY WHAT HE HAS SAID AND DONE AND PROMISED TO DO, AS WELL AS WHAT HE WANTS US TO DO AND NOT DO IN OUR LIVES.

That's nice, dear. But how do you actually know any of that? Where is the evidence to support any of those claims?

WHAT? IF GOD FELT HE NEEDED EVIDENCE TO PROVE HIS EXISTENCE, HE WOULD HAVE PROVIDED SOME. ARE YOU SO ARROGANT TO THINK THAT GOD SHOULD JUSTIFY HIS EXISTENCE AND PROVE HIMSELF TO US?

Ah, so you claim to have knowledge of something for which you also claim there can be no possible evidence. How very interesting!

COMMON SENSE ATHEISM

"Evidence #2"

The Ongoing Adventures of "Maude and Eugene" ™

THE ODDS OF COMPLEX LIFE EVOLVING BY RANDOM BLIND CHANCE ARE IMPOSSIBLY SMALL!

That's nice, dear. But if you actually read a science book instead of the Bible, you'd know that evolution involves the operation of non-random physical laws upon random events, which is not the same as random blind chance.

COMMON SENSE ATHEISM

"Evolution #1"

The Ongoing Adventures of "Maude and Eugene" ™

"EVOLUTIONISTS" ARE PEOPLE WHO PUT THEIR FAITH IN SCIENCE INSTEAD OF GOD!

That's nice, dear. But if you stopped reading creationist literature and actually paid attention to the rest of the world, you'd know that the vast majority of christians and other theists have no trouble accepting the truth of evolution.

COMMON SENSE ATHEISM

"Evolution #2"

"Evolution #3"

"Existence"

The Ongoing Adventures of "Maude and Eugene" ™

ATHEISTS CAN'T EXPLAIN HOW THE UNIVERSE BEGAN, SO IT'S ONLY LOGICAL TO BELIEVE THAT GOD DID IT!

Yes, dear. Of course, if you actually *knew* anything about logic you'd know that the lack of a better explanation doesn't somehow magically make your explanation more likely.

COMMON SENSE ATHEISM

"Explanation #1"

The Ongoing Adventures of "Maude and Eugene" ™

ATHEISTS AND "EVOLUTIONISTS" CAN'T EXPLAIN THE ORIGIN OF LIFE!

Yes, dear. Of course, theists and evolution deniers can't explain it either because **NOBODY** actually knows. Remember – "God did it" isn't actually an explanation; it's just an *assertion* unsupported by any evidence.

COMMON SENSE ATHEISM

"Explanation #2"

"Explanation #3"

"Explanation #4"

The Ongoing Adventures of "Maude and Eugene" ™

THERE ARE MANY THINGS THAT SCIENCE CANNOT EXPLAIN, INCLUDING THE ORIGIN OF THE UNIVERSE, THE ORIGIN OF LIFE AND THE EXISTENCE OF CONSCIOUSNESS, WHICH MEANS THAT GOD MUST BE THE EXPLANATION!

Yes, dear. Of course, most educated people understand that the opposite of "science *can* explain something" is "science *cannot* explain something" and not "therefore, God did it." Also, the fact that science cannot *currently* explain something doesn't mean it will *never* be able to do so.

COMMON SENSE ATHEISM

"Explanation #5"

The Ongoing Adventures of "Maude and Eugene" ™

I DON'T NEED PROOF OF GOD'S EXISTENCE BECAUSE I HAVE

FAITH

AND FAITH IS THE ONLY WAY TO KNOW ANYTHING FOR SURE!

Yes, dear. Of course, if faith were a valid way of knowing the truth then all religions would be equally true and all gods worshiped by anybody would be equally real, since everybody has faith.

COMMON SENSE ATHEISM

"Faith #1"

"Faith #2"

"Faith #3"

The Ongoing Adventures of "Maude and Eugene" ™

THE VARIOUS PHYSICAL CONSTANTS OF THE UNIVERSE ARE SO FINELY TUNED FOR THE EXISTENCE OF LIFE THAT THE ONLY EXPLANATION IS THAT GOD IS RESPONSIBLE!

Yes, dear. Except, of course, we don't know that the various "constants" could have had any other possible values. Plus, there's a huge difference between "capable of sustaining life" and "capable of sustaining life as we know it." Oh – and if the universe is supposedly "finely tuned" to support life, it seems awfully strange that the vast majority of the universe is not, in fact, actually capable of sustaining life. Besides, why focus just on life? The universe is equally "finely tuned" for the existence of black holes and diamonds and ringed planets and comets and pulsars and quasars and mountains...

COMMON SENSE ATHEISM

"Fine-Tuning"

The Ongoing Adventures of "Maude and Eugene" ™

EVERYTHING THAT BEGINS TO EXIST HAD A CAUSE. SINCE THE UNIVERSE BEGAN TO EXIST, IT MUST HAVE ALSO HAD A CAUSE. THIS PROVES THAT GOD EXISTS!

Yes, dear. Except, of course, we don't actually *know* that our observed laws of causality apply to the universe as a whole. And even if the universe *did* have a "cause," that doesn't mean the cause was necessarily your "God" or any god.

COMMON SENSE ATHEISM

"First Cause"

"Goalposts #1"

"Goalposts #2"

"Hatred"

"Ineffable"

The Ongoing Adventures of "Maude and Eugene" ™

IT'S INTELLECTUALLY DISHONEST FOR ATHEISTS TO REJECT GOD UNLESS THEY HAVE FIRST STUDIED AND UNDERSTOOD EVERY POSSIBLE CONCEPT OF GOD!

That's nice, dear. And did you do all that before deciding to *believe* in God?

DON'T BE SILLY! I BELIEVE BECAUSE MY PARENTS TOLD ME IT WAS TRUE.

COMMON SENSE ATHEISM

"Intellectual Dishonesty"

The Ongoing Adventures of "Maude and Eugene" ™

ATHEISTS ARE IRRATIONAL FOR DENYING GOD DESPITE NOT BEING ABLE TO PROVE THAT HE DOESN'T EXIST!

Yes, dear. And that's why you believe in demons and dragons, witches and warlocks, ghouls and goblins, banshees and bugbears, etc., right?

COMMON SENSE ATHEISM

"Irrational"

The Ongoing Adventures of "Maude and Eugene" ™

OF COURSE GOD IS ALL-LOVING, BUT JUSTICE DEMANDS THAT OUR SINS ARE PUNISHED, AND GOD'S MERCY ALLOWS US TO ESCAPE THAT PUNISHMENT IF WE CHOOSE TO ACCEPT IT.

Yes, dear. Of course, that totally ignores the fact that God is the one who would have set up the laws of justice in the first place. So remind me why, exactly, an "all-loving" God would set up a system where any violations of His laws would be punished with eternal torment?

COMMON SENSE ATHEISM

"Justice"

The Ongoing Adventures of "Maude and Eugene" ™

THE STORY OF NOAH'S ARK IS PERFECTLY PLAUSIBLE SINCE NOAH BROUGHT TWO OF EACH "KIND" OF ANIMAL INSTEAD OF TWO OF EACH SPECIES. SO JUST TWO CATS, TWO DOGS, TWO HORSES, ETC.

Yes dear. And then, of course, right after the ark landed those two "cats" began to speciate at a rate that would make an evolutionary biologist blush in shame (without anybody actually seeing it happen) in order to produce all the Lions, Tigers, Jaguars, Panthers, Leopards, Ocelots, Lynxes (Canadian, Iberian and Eurasian), House Cats (all the different breeds), Snow Leopards, African Golden Cats, Asian Golden Cats, Bobcats, Caracals, Chinese Desert Cats, Clouded Leopards, Fishing Cats, Servals, African Wild Cats, Andean Mountain Cats, Black-footed Cats, Bornean Bay Cats, European Wild Cats, Flat-headed Cats, Geoffroy's Cats, Iriomote Cats, Jaguarundi, Jungle Cats, Kodkods, Leopard Cats (different from leopards, mind you), Marbled Cats, Margays, Oncillas, Pallas Cats, Pampas Cat, Pumas (a.k.a Mountain Lions or Cougars), Rusty Spotted Cats and Sand Cats, etc., that we see today. You're right – that sounds sooooo much more plausible!

COMMON SENSE ATHEISM

"Kinds"

"Metaphorical #1"

"Metaphorical #2"

"Miracles"

"Morality"

The Ongoing Adventures of "Maude and Eugene" ™

ATHEISTS CAN'T BE GOOD PEOPLE BECAUSE THEY DON'T FEAR

DIVINE RETRIBUTION

AND THEREFORE HAVE NO REASON NOT TO LIE, STEAL, MURDER, RAPE, ETC.

Yes, dear. Of course, that argument would make a lot more sense if there weren't so many theists running around lying, stealing, murdering, raping, etc., despite supposedly having a fear of divine retribution. Perhaps a fear of divine retribution isn't actually required to be a good person after all?

COMMON SENSE ATHEISM

"Morality #2"

The Ongoing Adventures of "Maude and Eugene" ™

WITHOUT A BELIEF IN GOD AND A FEAR OF DIVINE RETRIBUTION, ATHEISTS ARE FREE TO MURDER AND RAPE AND LIE AND STEAL AS MUCH AS THEY WANT!

Yes, dear. Fortunately, though, the amount that most atheists actually *want* to murder and rape and lie and steal is "none." Unlike most theists, who apparently need a belief in God and a fear of divine retribution to stop them from doing those things, which says a lot more about theists than it does about atheists...

COMMON SENSE ATHEISM

"Morality #3"

"Negative"

"Newton"

The Ongoing Adventures of "Maude and Eugene" ™

ATHEISTS BELIEVE THAT **EVERYTHING** WAS CREATED FROM **NOTHING!**

Actually, dear, it's usually CHRISTIANS who think that the universe was created "out of nothing" (by God, of course). Atheists generally just say they don't know how the universe began. And remember -- "we don't know" does not mean "therefore God did it."

COMMON SENSE ATHEISM

"Nothing #1"

The Ongoing Adventures of "Maude and Eugene" ™

ATHEISTS ARE **IRRATIONAL** BECAUSE THEY BELIEVE IN **IMPOSSIBLE** THINGS, LIKE THE ENTIRE UNIVERSE JUST POPPED INTO BEING FROM **NOTHINGNESS!**

Actually, dear, it's usually CHRISTIANS who think that the universe was created "out of nothing." This doctrine even has an official name: "creatio ex nihilo" (literally, "creation from nothing").

OH, BUT THAT'S DIFFERENT! WE ALSO BELIEVE IN A GOD WHO CAN DO IMPOSSIBLE THINGS, SO THAT MAKES BELIEVING IN IMPOSSIBLE THINGS PERFECTLY RATIONAL....

COMMON SENSE ATHEISM

"Nothing #2" (a.k.a. "Impossible Things")

"Ontology"

"Order"

The Ongoing Adventures of "Maude and Eugene" ™

YOU SHOULD **CHOOSE** TO BELIEVE IN GOD JUST IN CASE HE EXISTS, SINCE YOU GAIN EVERYTHING IF YOU ARE RIGHT AND LOSE NOTHING IF YOU ARE WRONG. IT'S ONLY **LOGICAL**!

Yes, dear. Unless, of course, you choose the wrong god to believe in. Or choose the wrong religion worshiping the right god. Or god can actually tell when people are only faking belief.

COMMON SENSE ATHEISM

"Pascal"

The Ongoing Adventures of "Maude and Eugene" ™

MOST OF THE WORLD'S POPULATION THROUGHOUT HISTORY HAVE BELIEVED IN <u>SOME</u> SORT OF GOD, WHICH INDICATES THAT THERE PROBABLY IS SOME SORT OF DIVINE FORCE IN THE UNIVERSE AND ATHEISTS ARE DELUDED FOR NOT BELIEVING IN IT.

If you say so, dear. Of course, all those beliefs are so wildly different that all it really indicates is that humans have a tendency to make up stories about supernatural creatures and miraculous accounts of creation. Besides, since when is the truth a popularity contest?

COMMON SENSE ATHEISM

"Popularity #1"

"Popularity #2"

"Prayer"

The Ongoing Adventures of "Maude and Eugene" ™

GOD IS A MUCH MORE PROBABLE EXPLANATION FOR THE UNIVERSE THAN THINGS JUST HAPPENING BY CHANCE!

Yes, dear. Of course, that would make more sense if you actually *knew* how probable God was in the first place. Just how probable *is* an intelligent being composed of "pure spirit" that exists outside of time and space, anyway?

COMMON SENSE ATHEISM

"Probability"

The Ongoing Adventures of "Maude and Eugene" ™

JESUS FULFILLED HUNDREDS OF PROPHECIES CONTAINED IN THE OLD TESTAMENT, WHICH PROVES HE MUST BE **GOD!**

Yes, dear. Of course, the fact that a character in one set of fictional stories is said to have fulfilled prophecies in a *previous* set of fictional stories doesn't make any of those stories actually true.

COMMON SENSE ATHEISM

"Prophecies"

The Ongoing Adventures of "Maude and Eugene" ™

WITHOUT GOD, ATHEISTS CANNOT HAVE ANY PURPOSE OR MEANING IN THEIR LIVES!

Yes, dear. Except, of course, that atheists are free to define their <u>own</u> purpose and meaning in life if they choose to do so. And don't you think it's a bit sad that your purpose and meaning in life can only come from what your religious leaders <u>tell</u> you is the correct interpretation of the specific passages in the holy book of the particular god you worship?

COMMON SENSE ATHEISM

"Purpose"

The Ongoing Adventures of "Maude and Eugene" ™

THERE MUST BE A GOD, OTHERWISE WE HAVE NO *PURPOSE* IN OUR LIVES, NO *HOPE* FOR AN AFTERLIFE, NO *COMFORT* UPON THE DEATH OF LOVED ONES AND NO *SATISFACTION* THAT EVIL DEEDS WILL EVENTUALLY BE PUNISHED!

That's nice, dear. Of course, even if all that were true, it's really more of an argument for why you *want* God to exist than it is an actual argument for why God *does* exist. But whatever helps you sleep at night, I guess...

COMMON SENSE ATHEISM

"Reasons"

"Religion"

"Science"

The Ongoing Adventures of "Maude and Eugene" ™

SOPHISTICATED THEISTS LIKE ME KNOW THAT GOD IS NOTHING LIKE HOW HE IS DESCRIBED IN ANCIENT HOLY BOOKS!

How nice, dear. Of course, it seems a bit odd that God would be such a poor communicator or care so little about people knowing the truth about him that he would wait thousands of years for "sophisticated theists" like you to finally figure it out, don't you think?

COMMON SENSE ATHEISM

"Sophisticated"

The Ongoing Adventures of "Maude and Eugene" ™

GOD IS ALL-POWERFUL AND ALL-LOVING! THE ONLY REASON THERE IS SO MUCH SUFFERING IN THE WORLD IS BECAUSE ADAM AND EVE SINNED AND CAUSED THE NATURAL WORLD TO ENTER INTO A "FALLEN" STATE!

Yes, dear. Of course, I wonder who set up the system whereby the sins of two people could actually cause the entire world to enter a "fallen" state in the first place, hmmmmm?

COMMON SENSE ATHEISM

"Suffering #1"

The Ongoing Adventures of "Maude and Eugene" ™

GOD IS ALL-POWERFUL AND ALL-LOVING! THE ONLY REASON THERE IS SO MUCH SUFFERING IN THE WORLD IS BECAUSE GOD GIVES US FREE WILL AND DOESN'T WANT TO PREVENT US FROM EXERCISING THAT FREE WILL!

Yes, dear. Of course, human free will doesn't really explain things like natural disasters, genetic diseases, parasitical infections, cancers, the whole predator/prey dynamic, etc., does it? Maybe God just really likes watching cute little animals suffer and die in horrible ways...

COMMON SENSE ATHEISM

"Suffering #2"

The Ongoing Adventures of "Maude and Eugene" ™

ATHEISTS ARE IRRATIONAL FOR THINKING THERE IS NO GOD WHEN THEY CANNOT POSSIBLY SEARCH THE ENTIRE UNIVERSE!

Yes, dear. Of course, the "God" actually *worshiped* by anybody is described as having said and done and promised to do very specific things right here on Earth and not just "somewhere in the universe."

[I think they call that "moving the goalposts."]

COMMON SENSE ATHEISM

"Universe"

"Morality #4" (a.k.a. "The End")

Printed in Great Britain
by Amazon

65639254R00161